# Unreconstructed: *Vietnam to Iraq*

Teddy D. Bitner

This book is dedicated to the memory of my father,

Dwight D. Bitner Jr.
Squad Leader, E Company, 163rd Infantry Regiment, 41st
Infantry Division, Pacific Campaign, World War II

who, in his lifetime and with his brother soldiers, secured our freedom by giving their youth in the defense of our nation.

Back cover photo: Unattributed US Army photo. Colonel Teddy Bitner, 1997.

Maps:
*Westpoint Atlas*, US Military Academy
Department of Defense Briefing on Iraqi Freedom, April 4, 2003

Printed by:
Lulu Enterprises, Inc.
Morrisville, NC

Additional copies may be purchased at: www.lulu.com

# UNRECONSTRUCTED: *VIETNAM TO IRAQ*
**Teddy D. Bitner**

## Contents

# Introduction

*"Kind hearted people might of course think there was some ingenious way to disarm or defeat an enemy without too much bloodshed, and might imagine this to be the goal of the art of war. Pleasant as it sounds, it is a fallacy that must be exposed: war is such a dangerous business that the mistakes which come from kindness are the very worst."[1]*

Carl von Clausewitz

A couple of years ago, a well known college textbook publisher asked me to review a textbook designed for use in a history survey course. As I read the book, I was surprised by the factual errors and omissions, in particular about the events of the last forty years. When I pointed out errors to the publisher, they said "thanks" but made no changes and have not asked me to review a textbook since. After taking a hard look at the books I used in Western Civilization and American History classes, I began preparing short papers to correct obvious factual errors. Those papers grew into this book. The purpose of this book is to provide factual accounts of greater depth than normally encountered in college level history surveys for selected historical threads, in areas where general histories tend to take a politically correct view. My intent is to represent history as accurately as possible – warts and all (hence the title). Clearly, I state opinions and draw conclusions, but try to make sure the reader can separate the historical narrative from my views.

The contents are briefly summarized below:

---

[1] Carl von Clausewitz, *On War*, ed Micahel Howard and Peter Paret (Princeton, NJ: Princeton University Press, 1984), 75.

v

Chapter One, Vietnam, summarizes America's involvement in the Vietnam War, explores reasons why the United States lost and the impact of the war on the American psyche, as well as the people of Southeast Asia. The perspective on the war presented in Chapter One runs against the mainstream of current histories of Vietnam. However, as subsequent generations review the conduct of the war – the gross miscalculations and the stunning successes – I believe an accurate picture will emerge. It is my hope to contribute to that picture.

Chapter Two, The US, Israel and the Arabs, looks at the origins of the relationship between the United States and Israel, developing Arab nationalism and roots of the "War on Terror". America's involvement in the Middle East changed over time, from the 1950's through the 1990's as did the nature of Middle Eastern and Islamic politics. Failure to understand the shift from Arab nationalism to Islamic fundamentalism impeded American interests and the spread of democracy in the region.

Chapter Three, US, Central America and the 1980's discusses the United States' role in countering communist activity in Central America, including controversy, costs and benefits to both the United States and the region. American involvement in Central America was Ronald Reagan's application of the "Reagan Doctrine". The basic questions are – Was it successful? Was it worth it?

Chapter Four, Winning the Cold War, reviews the underlying American strategy for fighting the Cold War, Soviet perceptions and countermeasures to that strategy, and factors that brought the Soviet Union down. This chapter reviews President Reagan's initiatives against the USSR in some detail.

Chapter Five, Desert Storm summarizes causes of the war, how it was fought, its outcome and influence on future conflicts.

Chapter Six, Wars of the 1990's describes US involvement in Somalia, Bosnia, Kosovo, and the war with Al Qaeda that became our current "War on Terror".

Chapter Seven, Afghanistan, Iraq and the "War on Terror" delves into the background of Al Qaeda, the American perspective on terror during the 1990's, September 11th and subsequent battles in Afghanistan and Iraq.

Chapter Eight, Now and Then provides a few concluding observations about the nature of history and provides suggestions to aid the reader in separating history from myth in contemporary literature.

Appendices A; Myths of Vietnam and B; Myths of Iraq. These two appendices that review commonly repeated myths and legends about these wars and facts that refute those myths.

It is my desire that the reader finds these summaries helpful, and that they assist in putting the "War on Terror" in context. I strongly encourage readers to provide comments and suggestions for future editions of this volume.

I would like to especially thank Hannah and Miriam Bitner for their unselfish assistance in proofing drafts and "suggesting" urgent corrections. All that tuition money was put to good use.

Teddy Bitner<br>Raymore, Missouri, 2005

Figure 1 - Vietnam, the Final Days, 1975

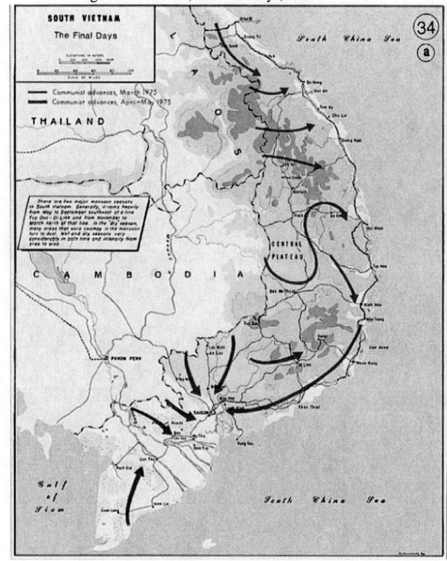

(*Westpoint Atlas*, United States Military Academy)

# Chapter One

# Vietnam

*"American soldiers do not lose wars.  Leaders lose wars."*

*"Victory is not a limited objective.  There is no other reason to engage an enemy, except victory."*

Major Mark Smith
Green Beret, Former POW[2]

On February 28, 1946, the Vietnamese communist revolutionary, Ho Chi Minh, sent a telegram to American President Harry Truman asking for US assistance in freeing Vietnam from their French overlords.  Vietnam, part of French Indo-China since October 1887, was occupied by the Japanese during World War II and the French government wasted no time after the war attempting to reestablish control of the region along with its rich resources.  President Truman never responded to the telegram, because he felt he needed to support his French wartime allies.  One of the "what if's" of history is: what if President Truman had answered Ho Chi Minh's telegram with "yes, we think you should be free, and I will help."?

## Vietnam – Independence from France

During World War II, the Office of Strategic Services (OSS), the forerunner of the Central Intelligence Agency (CIA),

---

[2] Danny "Greasy" Belcher reports of Major Mark Smith, "Mark Smith is a retired Special Forces (Green Beret) Major.  He was captured in the battle of Loch Ninh in Vietnam.  He had 38 holes in his body when captured, back broken, lung messed up, bowel penetrated, and other wounds.  He was held in a camp in Cambodia until released." August 17, 2005.

coordinated anti-Japanese activities with Ho Chi Minh and the Viet Minh guerillas. The Viet Minh (officially, the *"Viet Nam Doc Lap Dong Minh"*, or "League for the Independence of Vietnam") was a coalition of communist and nationalist organizations that opposed the Vichy French[3] and Japanese during World War II. OSS support included assisting Vietnamese opposition to the French Vichy puppet government that the Japanese allowed to continue during most of the war. Near the end of and after the war, Ho seized control of the Viet Minh movement and established a government in opposition to the French colonial administration. During the war, Ho expressed admiration for the United States, and wrote several letters to President Truman immediately following the war requesting assistance (the February 28, 1946 telegram is but an example). However, Ho Chi Minh was a communist, and a charter member of the French Communist Party founded in Paris in 1920. His political philosophy and practical approach were rooted in communism, not democratic tradition.

The British entered Vietnam immediately after World War II to restore order and French control using Indian troops, former French prisoners of war (who had been held by the Japanese) and even captured Japanese forces. British actions inevitably led to resistance by Ho and his Viet Minh forces. In 1945, and again in 1950, Ho declared himself head of the Democratic Republic of Vietnam. By 1950, he had lined up Soviet and communist Chinese support for his new government, and the war against the French escalated. By March 1954, the Viet Minh defeated the French, culminating in the Battle of Dien Bien Phu. In the war's aftermath, Vietnam was divided into two parts at a conference in Geneva. North Vietnam was placed under Viet Minh control while the Republic of Vietnam (South Vietnam), a new government formed in the south, had support from the British, French and American governments.

---

[3] Vichy is a city in France and the seat of the Nazi installed government after their invasion of France in 1940, thus France under German control was known as "Vichy"

2

Ho was not happy with the settlement and planned to gain control of the entire country.

## *America Goes to War*

America had an aversion to sending ground combat troops to fight in Asia. President Eisenhower's (President from 1953 to 1961) solution to the problem in Asia (particularly involving the communist Chinese) was to plan the employment of nuclear weapons in the event of a war, instead of sending ground troops. It is unknown whether Ho knew of Eisenhower's strategy, but during the 1950's, Ho limited his activities in South Vietnam to the infiltration of communist guerillas, mainly by sea. The Kennedy Administration, which took office in 1961, concluded that Eisenhower's approach was too heavy-handed and began to consider use of limited warfare instead of defaulting to a nuclear option. The unhappy experience of Korea notwithstanding, the Kennedy Administration (1961-1963) began contemplating deployment of ground troops to support the fledging South Vietnamese government. In 1961, President Kennedy sent General Maxwell Taylor[4] to assess the situation in Vietnam. Taylor recommended sending ground troops to support the South Vietnamese government and demonstrate to American allies in Southeast Asia her resolve to support her friends. Taylor's recommendation was reinforced by Administration officials such as Secretary of State Dean Rusk, who argued that the US was committed to fighting under the provisions of the Southeast Asian Treaty Organization (SEATO). Other leading Washington figures at the time, such as George Kennan (more on him in Chapter Four) believed that supporting the government of South Vietnam was not in the strategic interests of the United States,

---

[4] General Maxwell Taylor commanded 101st Airborne Division in World War II and was the UN Commander in Korea. He retired in 1959 from the Army, but was recalled to active duty in 1962 to serve as the Chairman of the Joint Chiefs of Staff. After his second retirement in 1964, he served as the US Ambassador to South Vietnam in 1964-1965.

3

nor was it important to maintaining America's reputation as a supporter of freedom.

However, there were domestic political reasons for getting involved in Vietnam. Republicans accused the Democratic Party (Kennedy's party) of "losing" China and eastern Europe to the communists during the Truman Administration (1945-1953) – so Presidents Kennedy (1961-1963) and Johnson (1963-1969) were sensitive to critics who labeled Democrats as soft on communists (even though President Truman had gone to war in Korea). Consequently, President Kennedy supported escalating American involvement in the war.

At the very beginning, President Kennedy made two decisions that haunted American involvement in Vietnam. The first was his attempt to obtain an end to fighting in Laos and removal of North Vietnamese troops from that country.

The North Vietnamese invaded and gained control of large amounts of Laotian territory next to North Vietnam in 1960 and 1961. In attempting to counter North Vietnamese activities and the communist insurgency in Laos, President Kennedy called for a peace conference in Geneva. The North Vietnamese agreed to attend the conference, but launched an offensive timed to take key objectives just as the cease fire took effect prior to start of the conference. Conference attendees signed a treaty on July 23, 1962 affirming the neutrality of Laos and calling for all foreign powers (including North Vietnam) to remove their troops. The North Vietnamese were required to withdraw their troops from Laotian territory by October 7, 1962, but on that date they ignored the deadline and had approximately 10,000 troops in Laos. North Vietnam began using Laos as a sanctuary for operations in South Vietnam in violation of the treaty, with the expectation that the Americans and South Vietnamese would not pursue them into "neutral" territory. Over the course of America's Vietnam War, Laos, Cambodia and North Vietnam became sanctuaries for North Vietnamese and Viet Cong forces – generally free from American and South Vietnamese ground pursuit. This became a prescription for defeat for America. The North Vietnamese also learned that the US was not willing to force them to abide by their treaty agreements.

President Kennedy's second major error regarding the course of American involvement in Vietnam resulted from his sanctioning of a coup against South Vietnamese President Diem. Diem was a devout Catholic and led a regime that actively repressed and persecuted Buddhists. Diem treated his political rivals harshly and charges of corruption tainted his regime. Kennedy was convinced that Diem could not unite the Vietnamese people to fight the communists. Through the CIA, Kennedy authorized Diem's removal – but not his assassination. However, Diem was assassinated on November 1, 1963 by the Vietnamese Army generals that removed him from power, just three weeks before President Kennedy's own death in Dallas. Kennedy's decision to remove Diem and his subsequent death at the hands of the South Vietnamese Army (ARVN) created chaos and confusion in South Vietnam and encouraged Ho to invade the south in 1964. Ho believed that he needed to invade and act quickly to take advantage of the instability in the South, before the Americans could react by committing large numbers of ground forces. Order was not effectively restored in South Vietnam until Nguyen Cao Ky became Premier in 1965.

In 1964, an encounter between the North Vietnamese and the US Navy in the Gulf of Tonkin touched off the official American involvement in Vietnam. In late July and August 1964, South Vietnamese commandos were involved in attacks along the North Vietnamese coast in the Gulf, provoking North Vietnamese gunboat activity. On August 2, the *USS Maddox* and *USS Turner Joy* were collecting intelligence in the Gulf. The official report indicates the US ships were in international waters, but Daniel Ellsberg[5], on duty in the Pentagon during at

---

[5] Daniel Ellsberg was a defense analyst who stole classified papers regarding the conduct of the war in Vietnam, photocopied them, and turned them over to the New York Times for publication in 1971. His

5

least a portion of the incident, claims that the US vessels were inside North Vietnamese territorial waters. North Vietnamese patrol boats attacked the ships. The aircraft carrier *U.S.S. Ticonderoga* sent aircraft to repel the North Vietnamese attackers and sank one boat, while damaging other enemy vessels. On the night of August 4, 1964, Captain John J. Herrick of the *Maddox* reported a second attack. The *Maddox* and the *Turner Joy* began firing at radar returns, but the captain later concluded that there probably were no enemy ships in the area.[6] James Stockdale (later a POW and Vice Admiral) who was in the air above the ships during the second incident and North Vietnamese General Nguyen Giap (senior commander of the North Vietnamese Army from the 1940's until their final triumph in 1975) have both indicated that no North Vietnamese patrol boats were involved in an attack on August 4. As a result of the real and purported incidents, President Johnson[7] sent a message to Congress on August 5 requesting a joint resolution to respond to the North Vietnamese attack. Specifically, the President laid out his propositions for Southeast Asia:

- America keeps her word. Here as elsewhere, we must and shall honor our commitments (under the Southeast Asia Treaty Organization)
- The issue is the future of Southeast Asia as a whole. A threat to any nation in that region is a threat to all, and a threat to us.
- Our purpose is peace. We have no military, political, or territorial ambitions in the area.

---

leak of what became known as the "Pentagon Papers" came well after public opinion had turned against the war, but helped fuel the call for ending American involvement.

[6] Patterson, Thomas G., J. Garry Clifford and Kenneth J. Hagan. *American Foreign Relations: A History Since 1895 (Fourth Edition).* (Lexington: D.C. Heath and Company, 1995), 410

[7] Critics later contended that President Johnson's Administration fabricated the Gulf of Tonkin incident to legitimize American involvement in Vietnam.

- This is not just a jungle war, but a struggle for freedom on every front of human activity. Our military and economic assistance to South Vietnam and Laos in particular has the purpose of helping these countries to repel aggression and strengthen their independence.[8]

Congress passed the *Tonkin Gulf Resolution*, which authorized the President to take any measures necessary, including the use of US armed forces, to assist any member of SEATO – in this case, South Vietnam.

Ironically, President Johnson expressed doubts about success in Vietnam as early as May 1964 in taped interviews with aides. He told his National Security Advisor, McGeorge Bundy, "[It] looks like to me that we're getting into another Korea. . . . I don't see what we can ever hope to get out of this." Vietnam was, Johnson said, "the biggest . . . mess that I ever saw.... It's . . . easy to get into a war, but ... it's going to be harder to ever extricate yourself if you get in."[9]

Regardless, President Johnson began to increase commitment of ground troops. In the spring of 1964, the US adopted the concept of graduated pressure (escalation). The idea was to respond to the North Vietnamese Army (NVA) and Viet Cong (VC - communist guerillas infiltrated into South Vietnam from the North) activities with increasing pressure, to "send a message" to the enemy.

American internal political pressure played an important part of the direction of the early part of the war.

Profoundly insecure, Johnson feared dissent and was obsessed with preventing damaging press leaks. In 1964 he

---

[8] "Tonkin Gulf Incident: 1964", *The Avalon Project at Yale Law School*, http://www.yale.edu/lawweb/avalon/tonkin-g.htm. Accessed July 21, 2005.
[9] H. P. McMaster, "President Johnson and the Joint Chiefs – Graduated Pressure." *Joint Force Quarterly*, Spring 2003.

was preoccupied with becoming President in his own right. Vietnam was principally seen as a danger to that end. After the election he feared congressional or public debate over Vietnam would jeopardize efforts to create the Great Society, his domestic legislative program. He could not risk failure. (Secretary of Defense Robert) McNamara would help the President protect his electoral chances and enact the Great Society by providing a Vietnam strategy that appeared cheap and could be pursued with minimal public and congressional scrutiny. The McNamara approach of graduated pressure would permit Johnson to pursue his objective of not losing the war while postponing the day of reckoning and preserving the illusion of continuity with the policies of previous administrations.[10]

## The Westmoreland Era

In 1964, the President sent General William Westmoreland to Vietnam. Westmoreland was a Westpoint graduate and served in World War II. After the war, he commanded a regiment in the 82nd Airborne Division, and commanded the 101st Airborne Division, and then the XVIII Airborne Corps. He became the youngest Major General in the US Army in 1956 at the age of 42. In Vietnam, General Westmoreland oversaw the troop buildup and first phase of America's war. His selection was to have momentous affect on the direction of the ground war. Westmoreland saw the war as a conventional struggle. He "concentrated on large-scale search-and-destroy operations that took place primarily in unpopulated and remote areas of the country"[11] and did not recognize the fact that North Vietnam's strength was in the villages and hamlets of South Vietnam – not in the NVA conventional regiments or Viet Cong battalions. Consequently, Westmoreland measured success by the destruction of enemy battalions (and body count), not by how

---

[10] Ibid.

[11] Lewis Sorely, *Thunderbolt: From the Battle of the Bulge to Vietnam and Beyond* (New York: Simon and Schuster, 1992), 192.

secure the country-side was for daily life. But Westmoreland's tenure was one of several factors that established the boundaries of the war for US forces. Another was the President's decision not to use Army reserve and National Guard units in the war – he did this because he was concerned that calling up the reserves would reach into the heartland of America and require widespread civil support for the war. Thus, the war was fought on the backs of active duty soldiers (volunteer and draftee) serving one year tours, instead of complete units rotating in and out of battle. "Permanantly" stationing combat units in country, and rotating soldiers through those units for one year tours created a contingency culture of survival for the troops and ticket punching for the officers. The result, over time, was the squandering of professionalism and honesty and replacing them with cynacism and careerism. Moral rot set in, enhanced by drugs and alcohol – but that would come later.

In May 1965, the 173$^{rd}$ Airborne Brigade deployed from Okinawa to Vietnam. They were follwed by the 1$^{st}$ Calvary Division, who in November 1965, conducted the first large scale ground force operation against NVA regular units in the Ia Drang Valley, as described in Hal Moore and Joe Galloway's book, *We Were Soldiers Once . . . And Young*. By 1967, troop levels in Vietnam stood approximately 450,000. Back in Washington, US Army Chief of Staff General Harold K. Johnson became increasingly convinced that Westmoreland's approach was not winning the war. Earlier (August 1965) – even before the Ia Drang Valley battle, General Johnson commissioned a study entitled "A Program for the Pacification and Long-Term Development of South Vietnam" (PROVN), to make recommendations on how to win the war. The study concluded that the real war was being fought in the villages, districts and provinces of Vietnam; not on large battlefields. The study indicated that Westmoreland failed to understand the nature of the conflict. During 1966, Secretary of Defense McNamara, attempting to fulfill President Johnson's wish to keep the war in the background, asked General Westmoreland for an assessment on what it would take to win the war. Westmoreland, instead of

9

using the PROVN results, commissioned his own study that concluded – based on his approach, that it would take one million Vietnamese, 500,000 Americans and ten years. Westmoreland recognized the political implications of this conclusion and resisted sending the report to McNamara. Caving into pressure from the Pentagon to provide some kind of answer, he eventually did send it, but with the caveat that he believed the war would be over by the summer of 1967.[12] In April 1967, Westmoreland told the Joint Chiefs of Staff that he needed an additional 201,250 soldiers to win the war – they were not impressed. Clearly something had to be done, and that something was General Creighton Abrams.[13] The White House announced on April 6, 1967 that Abrams (Westmoreland's Westpoint classmate) was going to Vietnam to be the Deputy Commander to General Westmoreland. The Army leadership intended for Abrams to eventually replace Westmoreland and change the direction of the war. The North Vietnamese had other ideas.

## Tet '68

The NVA and VC began the "Tet Offensive" on the night of January 29, 1968. Eventually, the offensive spread to the entire country as the communists intended to create a general anti-government uprising among the South Vietnamese population. Westmoreland had led the American people to believe that the war was virtually won, but "it was humiliating for Westmoreland

---

[12] Ibid., 193.

[13] General Creighton Abrams had a remarkable career. He graduated from West Point in 1936, commanded a tank battalion in World War II (including the Battle of the Bulge). Abrams served as chief of staff of various corps in Korea and commanded the 3rd Armored Division from 1960 to 1962. Before going to Vietnam, he was Vice Chief of Staff of the US Army. Upon his return, he became Chief of Staff. He died of cancer while serving in that position in September 1974. Abrams initiated a series of reforms that transformed the United States Army following Vietnam.

– he couldn't get out of his own headquarters."[14]  The North Vietnamese government totally committed to this attack, including the Viet Cong Infrastructure (VCI) in the south.  The VCI was established to act as a shadow government of South Vietnam – to control the villages and provinces and coerce the people to support the VC and NVA units with rice, sanctuary and information.  During Tet, the NVA and VC fought furiously, but they were doomed to fail – because the expected uprising never came.  One of the NVA's prime targets was the US Embassy building in Saigon.  Arriving in a truck and taxicab, VC entered the embassy compound, but their attack was quickly dealt with.

> Within five hours helicopters had landed American airborne troops onto the grounds.  The Americans killed all nineteen enemy infiltrators and secured the embassy.  The enemy assault, like dozens more that morning against President Nguyen van Thieu's palace and other Vietnamese and American buildings, was a complete surprise and yet failure at the same time.[15]

The image presented by the press of the action at the American Embassy, however, was not one of victory, but

> . . . dying Americans unable to protect the nerve center of their massive expeditionary force while their corrupt South Vietnamese allies shot the unarmed and innocent. . . As they watched their television sets, Americans wondered if victory really was at hand and were troubled over what and whom to believe.[16]

On the day of the VC embassy attack, photographer Eddie Adams took a Pulitzer Prize winning photograph of South Vietnamese General Nguyen Ngoc Loan shooting a captured VC infiltrator in the head.  The prisoner that Loan shot was part of a

---

[14] Sorely, 212.
[15] Victor Davis Hanson, *Carnage and Culture*, (New York: Anchor Books, 2002), 391.
[16] Ibid., 393.

11

team that killed several of Loan's security guard force, including one officer who was at home with his family. That photograph (referred to by Hanson in the quote above) was the image the press associated with Tet and the VC attack on the embassy. The American public was presented with a vision that Americans were killing innocents in the jungles and streets of Vietnam.

The first Tet eventually ended with the US Marines clearing the city of Hue on February 25. In the first week of the battle, the NVA and VC lost 32,204 confirmed killed and 5,803 captured. American losses were 1,015 killed, and South Vietnamese Army were 2,819 killed. Civilian casualties at the hands of the NVA and VC were over 7,000, and another 5,000 tortured and murdered. In Hue city, where the NVA held out the longest, over 2,800 grave sites were discovered with mutliated bodies of local teachers, doctors and political leaders. Approximately 2,000 other individuals "disappared" in Hue – their bodies were never found.

General Abrams stated that the South Vietnamese forces performed well during the battle, while the NCA, VC and VCI were broken. The North Vietnamese infrastructure in the south was in shambles. Even so, they were ordered to attack again in May, then again at the beginning of August. After the August attack NVA and VC forces were ordered to withdraw to sanctuaries in Laos and Cambodia. When they attempted to reenter South Vietnam, they encountered stiff resistence and found it difficult to reestablish themselves in the villages and hamlets. NVA units, in particular, encountered severe problems because the infrastructure was no longer there to support them. They continued to operate with difficulty through 1972, when American withdrawal was in full force. Tet was a significant military defeat for North Vietnam.

Readers of American newspapers or viewers of the evening news came away with a different opinion of Tet. General Westmoreland's insistance that America was winning the war before Tet (remember, he said the war would be over by the summer of 1967) indicated an incredible degree of incompentence at best, or outright deception at worst. To compound the situation, Westmoreland, along with the Chairman of the Joint Chiefs of Staff, General Wheeler requested an immediate, additional 206,000 troops be sent to Vietnam. The request, piled on top of Tet, was volcanic. The new Secretary of Defense, Clark Clifford remarked, "we seem to have a sinkhole."[17] Westmoreland was recalled and made Army Chief of Staff. General Abrams replaced him as the senior commander in Vietnam.

The public was treated to a declaration that the war was unwinnable by "the most trusted man in America", Walter Cronkite.[18] Optimistic predictions by General Westmoreland contrasted sharply with TV images of VC running amonk and attacking the US Embassy in Saigon. What should have been hailed as a major tactical victory was portrayed as a defeat by the media and confirmed by General Westmoreland's request for more troops.

And regarding the military and political aspects of Tet, it became a watershed event. Lewis Sorely writes:

Before Tet, the United States was building up its forces and bases in Veitnam, while afterward it was drawing them

---

[17] Ibid., 221

[18] Cronkite's *CBS Evening News* broadcast on February 27, 1968, concludes with: "To say that we are closer to victory today is to believe, in the face of the evidence, the optimists who have been wrong in the past. To suggest we are on the edge of defeat is to yield to unreasonable pessimism. To say that we are mired in stalemate seems the only realistic, yet unsatisfactory, conclusion. On the off chance that military and political analysts are right, in the next few months we must test the enemy's intentions, in case this is indeed his last big gasp before negotiations. But it is increasingly clear to this reporter that the only rational way out then will be to negotiate, not as victors, but as an honorable people who lived up to their pledge to defend democracy, and did the best they could."

down and redeploying men and units in wholesale lots. Before Tet, America was seeking a military victory in Vietnam, but after it she was seeking to get out – with whatever shreds of credit and dignity she might salvage, perhaps, but most of all to get out. Before Tet, the forces in Vietnam, despite a highly vocal and visible protest movement in the United States, retained a large reservoir of support and backing from the American people; after it, both left and right turned against the war in rapidly increasing numbers, and the most delicate task was to preserve some semblance of support while progressibvely disengaging. Before Tet, the cream of the Regular Army had led American forces; afterward, the experience level and maturity of the battlefield leadership spiraled downward. Until Tet, the forces in the field were in the main highly disciplined and professional; after it, they were increasingly wracked by problems of drug abuse, racial disharmony, internal dissent, and indiscipline, in part reflections of the rapidly changing climate at home. Before Tet, much of America thought we were winning the war; afterward, most considered it lost. And before Tet, it was Westmoreland's war; thereafter, it was up to Abrams to carry on.[19]

## The Abrams Era

As the new commander in Vietnam, General Abrams immediately put into place the recommendations of the PROVN study that had been completed three years earlier. After Tet, Abrams accelerated the US and South Vietnamese rural pacification program, by reclaiming hamlets and villages for the people and making it impossible for whatever VCI that might remain to operate effectively. These tactics undermined the communist political base in the south and forced Hanoi to conduct conventional military operations without local support, where they would be at a distinct disadvantage. Abrams' efforts were so successful that in 1969 and 1970, most of South

---

[19] Sorely, 220.

Vietnam was considered secure for the Vietnamese people. However, American political realities soon undid this work.

The Tet Offensive, followed by Walter Cronkite's comments, took the wind out of President Johnson's 1968 campaign. On March 31, 1968, President Johnson announced that he would not run for president. Richard Nixon, the Republican candidate, claimed that he had a secret plan to end the war. When Nixon won, Vietnamization of the war was already well under way by General Abrams, but political pressure accelarated the process. North Vietnam realized that they could wait out the United States.

In March 1970, Cambodian General Lon Nol ousted Prince Sihanouk as head of Cambodia and demanded that the North Vietnamese withdraw from Cambodian within 72 hours. Lon Nol requested US assistance in removing North Vietnamese forces from Cambodian territory. North Vietnam backed the *Khmer Rouge*[20] (officially known as the "Communist Party of Cambodia") against the new regime. As a test of the Vietnamization process and an attempt to deny access to staging basis to the NVA, Abrams decided to conduct an extended raid into Cambodia in April 1970. Performance of South Vietnamese units was mixed (some good, some bad with the senior leadership being awful), but the raid netted huge amounts of stockpiled supplies and destroyed a number of NVA basecamps. However, back in the United States the "Cambodian Incursion" caused a firestorm of protest. President Nixon decided to speed up the withdrawal of US units.

In 1972, the NVA tried again with their "Easter Offensive", another conventional force attack into South Vietnam from sanctuaries primarily in Cambodia. At that time, only two US combat brigades and one South Korean division remained of the

---

[20] The *Khemer Rouge* was ultimately responsible for the deaths of between 1.2 to 3 million Cambodians during their reign of terror from 1975 until their removal from power by Vietnam in January 1979.

allied forces formerly in South Vietnam. Consquently, the brunt of the battle fell on ARVN units. The NVA collected teenagers to fill their ranks and committed their entire army to the fight – leaving North Vietnam virtually undefended. The NVA launched their attack with 14 infantry divisions, 26 separate infantry regiments and three armor regiments. Tankers in the armor regiments were recent graduates of the Soviet tank school and manned T-54 and T-55 tanks with 100 milimieter main guns – much more powerful and effective than the M48 American tanks then operating in South Vietnam. Hanoi had deep cover agents inside the South Vietnamese Army that were employed during this offensive. One commander, who was an agent, surrendered his entire unit. However, the NVA offensive failed due to a combination of effective South Vietnamese defense and US bombing. The NVA were unable to attempt another offensive until 1975, when they restocked and rebuilt their armed forces for the final push. American and South Vietnamese defensive efforts during the Easter Offensive demonstrated that South Vietnam could indeed be defended using South Vietnamese ground forces supported by US air power.

## *Extraction and Defeat*

On Januaray 27, 1973, five years after Tet, parties in the war reached an agreement in Paris. To get the South Vietnamese to go along with the settlement, the United States promised three things: military assistance if the South Vietnamese needed it, one-for-one replacement of equipment lost or destroyed in combat, and American economic assistance to South Vietnam. The peace agreement required the US to remove military forces from South Vietnam (but the North Vietnamese didn't have that requirement) and the simultaneous release of American prisoners of war.

By January 1975, the Soviet supplied NVA was the fifth largest conventional army in the world. The Ho Chi Minh trail, created as a result of President Kennedy's treaty on Laos in 1962 was now paved and moving supplies and equipment unimpeded from port to dumps and staging areas along the border. On March 10, 1975, the final North Vietnamese offensive began (see Figure 1). With conventional forces, their invasion of South Vietnam resulted in the fall of the Saigon government. Unlike Nixon's reaction during the 1972 Easter Offensive, the Ford Administration (1974-1977) did not respond to South Vietnamese requests to honor commitments made at the time of the Paris Peace Accords two years earlier. Congress had, in fact, voted to curtail funds for American support to South Vietnam. The ARVN, starved for ammunition, equipment and other supplies, was unable to stop the NVA, which was bountifully supplied by the Soviet Union and communist China. On April 30, 1975, Saigon fell to the communists, and American's longest war was over.

## Cost of the War

Regarding the human cost of the war, the communist Vietnamese government released the following statemet in 1995:

The Hanoi government revealed on April 4 that the true civilian casualties of the Vietnam War were 2,000,000 in the north, and 2,000,000 in the south. Military casualties were 1.1 million killed and 600,000 wounded in 21 years of war. These figures were deliberately falsified during the war by the North Vietnamese Communists to avoid demoralizing the population.[21]

US casualties were over 58,000 killed, 300,000 wounded and over 2,000 missing in action. South Vietnamese military casulaties were 223,000 killed and 1,170,000 wounded and North Vietnamese and VC 1,100,000 killed and 600,000 wounded. But American prestige, honor and reliability were also casualties of the Vietnam War. American enemies reveled in her defeat.

---

[21] "Vietnamese Government Release of Official Figures", *The Agence France Presse (French Press Agency)* news release of 4 April 1995

The North Vietnamese immediately set about to "reeducate" the South in proper communism. They used "thought reform", resettlement, surviellance and education. Hundreds of thousands of former government officials, military personnel, religious and labor leaders, teachers, intellectuals and lawyers were sent off to reeducation camps. In 1985, Hanoi admitted to still having approximately 10,000 in reduction camps, but independent estimates make that number as high as 40,000. University of California at Berkley demographer Jacqueline Desbarat's conservative estimate of executions in post-war Vietnam stands at 65,000, which is approximately 1/3 of the total possible, taking into account eyewitness testimony of Vietnamese refugees in the United States and France. Desbarat's figures do not include those that died of starvation, disease, exhaustion, suicide or injuries sustained by prisoners while clearing minefields. Approximately 2,000,000 people attempted to escape from Vietnam in the years after the war. The spread of communism to neighboring Cambodia resulted in a devastating genocide led by Pol Pot. Estimates of the number killed by Pol Pot's *Khmer Rouge* from 1975 to 1979 range from 1.2 million (US State Department) to 1.7 million (government of Cambodia) to 3 million (Cambodian Government in exile). Ironically, Pol Pot's regime ended when the communist government of Vietnam invaded to put an end to the killing.

## The Anti-War Movement

The "Anti-War" movement in the United States was an outgrowth of pre-existing radical political groups such as the Students for a Democratic Society (SDS), an organization dominated by Marxist philosophy; and the Free Speech Movement (FSM), an organization at the University of Califirnia at Berkley initially involved in the Civil Rights Movement. The anti-war "movement" began to coalesce on college campuses beginning in 1965, fueled by college students' fear of the draft.

Initial objections (1965) to the war centered on the draft and a call for alternate service options for objectors. Later, as Civil Rights leaders such as Martin Luther King became involved (1966-1967), criticism became multi-faceted with the charge that the war was draining resources away from domestic intiatives, such as President Johnson's Great Society. This criticism was, in fact, exactly what President Johnson sought to avoid, by attempting to gradually escalate the war in 1964 and deliberately not mobilizing the American public behind the war. Finally, the movement shifted to a moralistic, pro-communist phase that portrayed the United States as an oppressor, US military personnel as war ciminals and the Vietnamese communists as downtrodden people yearning for freedom. This latter stage is the era of Jane Fonda and John Kerry.

The anti-war movement gained momentum after Tet 68 and was reinforced with news of the Cambodian incursion, the deaths of protestors at Kent State University in Ohio by National Guard troops, and the revelations about a massacre in the village of My Lai in 1968. Later, Daniel Ellsberg's leak of the "Pentagon Papers" to the *New York Times* further encouraged the movement and lent credibility to their claims. As the third phase of the anti-war movement kicked in, it's leadership shifted from the SDS, FSM and other relatively well organized groups to a range of loose knit and less organized elements, with a distinctly hippie flavor. The portion of the movement that focused on allegations that US soldiers were actively and routinely involved in war crimes, was supported by information generated by the World Peace Council. The WPC was formed in 1949 and funded by the KGB (Soviet secret police and intelligence organization). The WPC, which became the bedrock source for disinformation employed by elements of the anti-war movement related to allegations of widespread American atrocities, is described by Ion Pacepa, former acting chief of the Romanian intelligence service, (thus well placed to know the details of the WPC and KGB relationship):

19

The KGB organized a vitriolic conference in Stockholm to condemn America's aggression, on March 8, 1965, as the first American troops arrived in South Vietnam. On Andropov's (Chief of the KGB) orders, one of the KGB's paid agents, Romesh Chandra, the chairman of the KGB-financed World Peace Council, created the Stockholm Conference on Vietnam as a permanent international organization to aid or to conduct operations to help Americans dodge the draft or defect, to demoralize its army with anti-American propaganda, to conduct protests, demonstrations, and boycotts, and to sanction anyone connected with the war. It was staffed by Soviet-bloc undercover intelligence officers and received about $15 million annually from the Communist Party's international department — on top of the WPC's $50 million a year; all delivered in laundered cash dollars.[22]

The first meeting of the Stockholm Conference was followed by others, and by Bertrand Russell's Citizens Commission of Inquiry (CCI), which had a similar purpose and connections.

After returning from service in Vietnam, John Kerry traveled to Paris in May 1970 on his honeymoon and met with the Viet Cong foreign minister Madame Nguyen Thi Binh at the Paris peace negotiations. At the time of his meeting with her, he was apparently a naval reserve lieutenant (raising interesting legal questions about meeting with the enemy during wartime). In June 1970, Kerry joined Vietnam Veterans Against the War (VVAW) and began taking part in various anti-war activities, many of which were funded by Jane Fonda. His testimony before Senate Foreign Relations Committee on behalf of the VVAW on April 22, 1971 included a description of American atrocities in Vietnam: that American soldiers had "personally raped, cut off ears, cut off heads, taped wires from portable

---

[22] Ion Pacepa, "Kerry's Soviet Rhetoric: The Vietnam-era Anti-War Movement Got Its Spin from the Kremlin", *National Review*, February 26, 2004.

20

telephones to human genitals and turned up the power, cut off limbs, blown up bodies, randomly shot at civilians, razed villages in fashion reminiscent of Genghis Kahn . ." Kerry indicated that these acts were not isolated; but were routine, widespread, and sanctioned by the military chain of command. Kerry also stated that North Vietnamese reprisals against the South following the war would be "far, far less than the 200,000 a year who are murdered by the United States of America." In July 1971, Kerry called a news conference at which he urged President Nixon to accept Madame Bihn's plan for ending the war – which included a deal that would return American POW's, in exchange for US withdrawal from Vietnam.[23]

Regarding Kerry's contention that atrocities were widespread and routine, there are actually only two documented cases of atrocities committed by US troops during the war. In both cases, a court-martial was conducted and defendants were found guilty (one was at My Lai in March 1968, the other at Song Thang-4 in February 1970). Declarations such as Kerry's echoed propaganda produced by the WPC and were demoralizing to the soldiers on the field and the soldiers about to go to Vietnam. In a circular produced by the North Vietnamese Government in 1971, direct contact with the anti-war movement through the Viet Cong delegation in Paris is specifically discussed.[24] This and other documents also describe the coordination of anti-war activities (in particular, the VVAW) in the spring and fall of 1971.

Jane Fonda is the daughter of actor Henry Fonda. Her anti-war activities came into the public consciousness in 1970 with her support of the VVAW and similar organizations. She is best know for her trip to North Vietnam in 1972, where she posed on

---

[23] John E. O'Neill and Jerome R. Corsi, *Unfit for Command: Swift Boat Veterans Speak Out Against John Kerry*, (Washington DC: Regnery Publishing Inc., 2004), 127.

[24] "Circular on Anti-War Movements in the US", 12-1370-71, People's Republic of Vietnam, undated (internal evidence indicates summer of 1971).

an anti-aircraft gun, made anti-American radio broadcasts on Radio Hanoi and met with American POWs. One POW, Michael Benge was asked by his keepers if he would meet with Miss Fonda. When he replied that he would really like to tell her about the conditions under which POWs were being held, he was made to kneel on a rocky floor for three days with a steel bar placed on his outstretched hands. Whenever his arms dropped, he was beaten with a bamboo rod.[25] Fonda's activities resulted in her being labeled "Hanoi Jane" and greatly reviled among American veterans. As a result, the image of her sitting on the anti-aircraft gun became an enduring icon for the anti-war movement.

Many veterans claim that the anti-war movement encouraged the enemy to continue the war (thus costing additional American lives and keeping POWs captive longer) and contributed to America's loss of the war – along with the attendant atrocities committed by the communists after the war.

## *The Media*

Tet '68 underscored the importance of the media in war. It was an American battlefield victory that gutted the NVA and VC – but was turned into a strategic defeat by Walter Cronkite's statements and media coverage at home. To be sure, General Westmoreland's confident optimism before Tet didn't help, but the media spun the story. Within a week, factual assessments of the battle became available, but it was too late.

Erin McLaughlin, in researching the impact of the media on the war, provides an excellent, factual summary:[26]

---

[25] Michael Benge addressed the issue of Jane Fonda's visit in a letter dated April 28, 1999.
[26] Erin McLaughlin, "Television Coverage of the Vietnam War and the Vietnam Veteran. http://www.warbirdforum.com/media.htm. Accessed July 27, 2005.

By the fall of 1967, 90 percent of the evening news was devoted to the war and roughly 50 million people watched television news each night (Bonior, Champlin, Kolly, 1984, p.4-5). Up until this time, the war had strong support from the media, the public, and Congress. The military continuously reported that the U.S was making encouraging progress. Gradually, however, support for the war began to decrease. Because no military censorship was established, journalists could follow the military into combat and report their observations without formal censorship. Thus, as journalists saw more grisly combat, they presented the public with more graphic images. Also, for the first time, interviewed soldiers expressed their frustration with the progress of the war.

Support began to decrease in the fall of 1967, but the major turning point in television's coverage of the war occurred during the Tet Offensive in late January 1968. Though North Vietnamese soldiers swept through more than one hundred Southern Vietnamese cities, Tet was actually a U.S victory because the North suffered enormous casualties. Television, however, portrayed the attack as a brutal defeat for the U.S; the media, not the military, confirmed the growing perception that the U.S. was unable to win the war. The percent of television stories in which journalists editorialized news jumped from 5.9 percent before Tet to 20 percent in the two months after (Hallin, 1986, p.170). The most significant statement came from the "most trusted man in America", Walter Cronkite. In a *CBS* special, Cronkite concluded, 'To say that we are closer to victory today is to believe, in the face of the evidence, the optimists who have been wrong in the past to say that we are mired in a bloody stalemate seems the only realistic, yet unsatisfactory conclusion" (Hallin, 1986, p.170). After the Tet Offensive and Cronkite's statement, coverage of American involvement in the war became predominantly negative. Before Tet, journalists described 62 percent of their stories as victories for the United States, 28 percent as defeats, and 2 percent as inconclusive. After Tet, 44 percent of the battles were deemed victories, 32 percent defeats, and 24 percent inconclusive (Hallin, 1986, p.161-162). Combat scenes were also more graphic. Films of civilian casualties increased from a pre-Tet average of 0.85 times per week to an average of 3.9 times per week. Films of military casualties also jumped from 2.4 to 6.8 times per week (Hallin, 1986, p.171). The most negative change in coverage was the portrayal of the U.S troops. Before the Tet Offensive, there were four television stories devoted entirely to the positive morale of the troops and zero negative stories. After Tet, two and a half stories mentioned positive morale while the number of negative morale stories increased to fourteen and a half (Hallin, 1986, p.180). Most of these negative references included increasing drug use, racial conflict, and disobedience among the U.S. soldiers.

Television coverage of the massacre at My Lai was perhaps the most damaging image for the U.S soldier's reputation. Though initial reports stated that the operation killed 100 enemy soldiers in March 1968, it was revealed a year later that First Lt. William Calley and his taskforce had killed up to 350 South Vietnamese civilians (Hammond, 1998, p.192). The massacre and Lt. Calley's trial became one of the war's leading stories. Moreover, it introduced the subject of American war crimes into television's remaining coverage of the war.

The intensely negative coverage of the war influenced both politicians and the public. Americans depended on television to see and understand the war, but the death and destruction they saw appeared as irrational killing when prospects for the war became increasingly negative. Therefore, the majority of Americans withdrew their support for the war after the Tet Offensive. War coverage declined from 90 percent of all newscasts to 61 percent from Richard Nixon's election through February 1969 (Bonior, Champlin, Kolly, 1984, p.7). Though the media had been covering the anti-war movement before 1968, it now overshadowed the war itself. Draft-card burning and demonstrations provided television with fresher conflict, human impact, and moral issues. With the massive loss of public support for the war, politicians initiated withdrawal policies. Television no longer focused on combat, but on the political process. From 1965 to 1969, the percentage of combat stories had been 48 percent; from 1970 until the end of U.S involvement, only 13 percent of news stores involved soldiers in combat (Bonior, Champlin, Kolly, 1984, p.8). Thus, Bonior, Champlin, and Kolly (1984, p.16) best sum up the damage done to the Vietnam veteran's image: In the rush to declare the Vietnam War over through stories on Vietnamization and the Paris Peace Talks, in the rush to judgment without second thought on Tet, in the rush to avoid controversy at any cost, the U.S public was left with one climactic image of their soldiers in Vietnam - losing the Tet Offensive while massacring civilians at My Lai.

## *Conclusion*

The assumption that America could not have won the war in Vietnam is prevalent today. But could we have won? Even with the blunders of the early years, the efforts to implement PROVN in conjunction with repeatedly failed NVA attempts to invade South Vietnam suggest that the war was winnable. Should we have gone to war in Vietnam in the first place? That sounds like a good topic for classroom debate!

Various groups of people reached the same conclusion about the direction of the war in Vietnam – but took widely divergent approaches based on their conclusions. For example, President Johnson confided his concern to members of his Administration about getting drawn into a war in Vietnam, General Harold Johnson (Army Chief of Staff) believed the war was going in the wrong direction and initiated the PROVN study to figure out how to fix it, Daniel Ellsberg (who leaked the "Pentagon Papers" to the *New York Times*) also came to believe that the US could not win as did Walter Cronkite, the most trusted man in

America. How each of these individuals responded to the same conclusion is a case study in individual and organizational behavior. The President pushed ahead, hoping to minimize the impact of the war on his Great Society, the American economy, and his chances for reelection in 1968. General Johnson began a campaign to change how the war was being conducted – convinced that an aggressive change in approach could result in a secure South Vietnam. Daniel Ellsberg (and many like him) took the opposite view of General Johnson – that the war was un-winnable and immoral, and that he had to expose what he believed to be the immoral conduct of the American government. Cronkite went on the evening news and declared that a stalemate was the best possible outcome. Four individuals – four responses. President Johnson, mired down in Washington politics and thinking inside the "containment" box convinced himself that the war needed to be fought, and that he could do so "on the cheap". Daniel Ellsberg released his papers in the midst of the third wave anti-war movement, giving support to the movement and encouraging the enemy to persevere. Walter Cronkite simply ignored the facts. He knew as well as anyone the overall situation in Vietnam, and that the North Vietnamese were a broken force, but clearly made a conscious decision to declare the war a stalemate – thus un-winnable. General Johnson took a constructive approach. Knowing that American and Vietnamese lives were invested in the future of Vietnam, he sought a solution for victory.

Vietnam was complex and deadly. In the war's aftermath, the communist government subjected the Vietnamese people to repression, violence, poverty and retribution – that at this writing still has not run its course. Millions died in Cambodia as a result of a brutal communist regime that came to power after the war. Other millions were displaced and tried to make their way to freedom thereby greatly enriching the population of the United States with Vietnamese and Cambodian refugees.

Vietnam veterans, as a group, have not turned into the predicted psychopaths (an expectation fueled by John Kerry's testimony about widespread, routine atrocities), but have flourished, even though they were initially shunned by many older veterans. In a curious turn of events, some who did not serve became "wannabees" – fake heroes pretending to have served in Vietnam and spinning stories for family and friends. However, as in every war, there are some veterans that have had difficulty returning to civilian life. They too, are victims of the war.

At the close of the war, over 2,000 American servicemen remained missing in action (MIA). Families of the missing, particularly those servicemen that were seen alive sometime after their capture by fellow prisoners of war (POW), retained hope that their loved ones would be returned after the release of the POWs. Over time, families organized, and with supporters, created the POW-MIA movement. For many years, groups within the POW-MIA movement were largely marginalized by the US government. However, in 1991, the Senate convened a special committee to review documentation and take testimony regarding reports of live POW sightings after the war. Senator John Kerry concluded that the reports (including sworn testimony from three former Secretaries of Defense; James Schlesinger, Melvin Laird and Elliot Richardson)[27] were false or inconclusive and greatly discredited the movement. However, a series of reports entitled the *The Gulag Study* prepared by the Defense POW/Missing Personnel Office concluded that live Americans were held by the Soviet Union in Gulags following several wars.[28] This series is an ongoing effort to uncover information from eyewitness testimony and Soviet archives. The POW-MIA movement was instrumental in getting legislation passed and contributing to a commitment within the military to recover POWs in future wars. This effort resulted, in part, in the recovery in Iraq of the first POWs in combat since World War II.

---

[27] Sydney H. Schanberg, "When John Kerry's Courage Went M.I.A." *Village Voice*, February 24, 2004
[28] Michael E. Allen, *The Gulag Study (Fifth Edition),* Defense POW/Missing Personnel Office, February 11, 2005.

The United States Army was morally and materially devastated by the war. When General Abrams left Vietnam to become the Army Chief of Staff, he faced the tremendous task of trying to revitalize a beaten service. But, Abrams put the Army back on the road to recovery through a series of initiatives to strengthen the moral fiber of the Army, improve the quality of leadership and training, and acquire the best equipment. Beyond troops and equipment, the Army began to take a critical look at how the war was conducted. Colonel Harry Summers wrote *On Strategy: A Critical Analysis of the Vietnam War*, a US Army War College study that assessed the tactical and strategic conduct of the war – concluding that it could have been won on the battlefield after all. He contended that the Army had become hide-bound by bureaucratic functionaries focused on moving mountains of materials and filling out forms – not on fighting and winning a war. His analysis took the Army back to the basics, using Carl von Clausewitz'[29] elements of warfare as a starting point. Summers' analysis was revolutionary, and provided a basis for future military thought and operations. The fruit of Abrams' and Summers' labor was the US Army in "Desert Storm".

American enemies and allies watched as the US consistently failed to enforce the treaty obligations of the North Vietnamese – the Laotian Treaty negotiated by President Kennedy and the Paris Peace Accords. In the end, the United States failed to live up to the obligations it made to the South Vietnamese people in getting their officials to agree to the Paris Accords.

And then, there is the American psyche. Each subsequent commitment of troops was compared in some respect to Vietnam – whether as a warning not to get involved in a developing situation, or as a declaration by a President that we had put Vietnam behind us as a nation. But what had we put behind us?

---

[29] Clausewitz was a Prussian military philosopher who wrote the highly influential book *On War* in response to Prussian military failures during the Napoleonic wars. *On War* became standard reading within the US Army in the years following Vietnam.

Summers, in a subsequent book, *On Strategy II: A Critical Analysis of the Gulf War* recalled the confidence that the world had in the United States prior to Vietnam by quoting the former South Vietnamese ambassador to the United States who said their "faith in the U.S. was total simply because . . they thought that the powerful and disinterested U.S. could not be wrong, and all the more so because the U.S. had never lost a war in its history."[30] Vietnam destroyed this trust around the world, and nowhere more greatly than among Americans.

---

[30] Harry Summers, *On Strategy II: A Critical Analysis of the Gulf War*, (New York: Dell, 1992), 8.

# Chapter Two

# The US, Israel and the Arabs

*"All men dream; but not equally. Those who dream by night in the dusty recesses of their minds wake in the day to find that all was vanity, but the dreamers of the day are dangerous men for they may act their dream with open eyes and make it possible. This I did."*

T. E. Lawrence

During World War I, the British cultivated friendships with Arab leaders in order to obtain their aid to overthrow the Ottoman Empire, which entered the war on the German side. Lieutenant Colonel T. E. Lawrence[31], popularly known as "Lawrence of Arabia", was instrumental in pushing the Arabs into the British camp and prodding the British government to help the Arabs achieve independence from their Turkish overlords. The results were the Arab revolt in 1916 and encouragement of Arab nationalism. The British promised independence, and although certain Arab tribes did obtain considerable territory, the British and French claimed title to what would become Iraq, Palestine, Trans-Jordan, Syria and Lebanon – occupying the vacuum created by the destruction of the Ottoman Empire at the end of the war. With justification,

---

[31] Born Thomas Edward Chapman, the family changed their name to Lawrence after his father abandoned them. Lawrence was an Oxford graduate and archeologist who joined the British Army at Cairo in 1914. In 1916, he worked with Arabs to coordinate an uprising against the Ottoman Empire that was ultimately successful. Lawrence strongly supported the cause of Arab nationalism and represented their interests at the Paris peace conference following the war. Eventually, in order to escape notoriety, he changed his name to J. H. Ross and served as an enlisted man in the Royal Air Force. He changed his name again to T. E. Shaw in 1923. Lawrence was killed in a motorcycle accident in 1935. His best known work is *The Seven Pillars of Wisdom* published in 1935.

Arab leaders were angered at the Western powers for drawing borders and creating countries without regard to tribal or cultural relationships.

A further complication created by British promises dealt specifically with Palestine. The *Sykes-Picot Agreement* of May 16, 1916, divided territories between direct British and French control, and areas of influence between the two countries. Palestine, which was created from "southern Syria" by the agreement, was left under international control for future consideration, but the *Balfour Declaration* of 1917 promised to create a Jewish national home in Palestine – these two documents were in direct conflict. The *Sykes-Picot Agreement* later expanded to benefit Italy and Russia, was kept secret until Vladimir Lenin, leader of the new Soviet Union (and thus privy to agreements made by the former Russian government), released the contents after the World War I resulting in considerable embarrassment among parties who planned to carve up the Middle East.

Between World War I and World War II, Arab nationalism or pan-Arabism began to gain greater strength in response to British rule. That coupled with conflicting claims on Palestine created tensions and shaped expectations. But British challenges weren't limited to Arab nationalists – they also had to deal with a growing Jewish problem as well. An expanding Jewish population (largely through immigration) drew an immediate and violent Arab reaction. A series of riots began in 1920 and culminated in the "Great Uprising" in the 1930's in which Arabs targeted British and Jewish interests alike.

When Jewish persecution began in Nazi Germany during the 1930's, many Jews attempted to leave Germany, but they found they were generally not welcome in the United States and several other countries. Some tried to immigrate to Palestine, and ironically, the Nazi's even attempted to help settle Jews there to remove them from Germany. However, responding to Arab resistance to Jewish immigration, the British government issued a White Paper designed to gain Arab support by restricting Jewish immigration to Palestine. Consequently, many Jews were returned to Germany, and went to their deaths in concentration camps. Jews living in Palestine at the time were faced with a choice – support the British in their fight against Hitler, or fight the British. This dilemma continued until near the end of the war, when it was obvious the Allies would defeat Germany – and leaders of radical Zionist groups stepped up their war with Britain.

On November 29, 1947, the United Nations General Assembly approved a plan to partition Palestine into Jewish and Arab states. Their decision resulted in heavy fighting between what had been an underground Jewish militia and Arabs. Fighting continued through May, 1948 when the State of Israel was declared – and the real war began. Troops from Lebanon, Syria, Iraq, Egypt, Trans-Jordan, Saudi Arabia and Yemen invaded Israel. Ultimately, Israel defeated the combined Arab force and separate cease fire agreements were signed with Arab states throughout 1949.

## *The Suez Crisis*

From 1949 to 1956 (the next Arab-Israeli War), the Cold War commingled with Middle Eastern politics. The United States, Great Britain and France supported Israel while the Soviet Union took the Arab side. In each case, support meant aid in weapons and funds.

Gamal Abdel Nasser seized control of Egypt in 1954 with the intent of uniting the Arab world (Arab nationalism) as an independent entity under his leadership. Nasser was an Egyptian Army Lieutenant Colonel and a leader in the "Free Officers Movement" that overthrew the British friendly Egyptian king in 1952 and then arrested the first president of Egypt in 1954. After taking control, he began to create an Arab block (like the Soviet block) fed by Arab nationalism and non-aligned with the great powers. But Nasser was forced to deal with the West and the Soviet Block to finance his development projects and to purchase arms. Nasser attempted to buy weapons from the US, but the Eisenhower Administration turned him down, so he approached the Soviet Union. The Soviets arranged a sale through Czechoslovakia.[32] Nasser was also looking for financing for the Aswan Dam project – a giant project to control the Nile River and create electricity. John Foster Dulles, the US Secretary of State, initially said the US would support the effort, but then backed away from the deal. These factors, along with US and British attempts to isolate Egypt and restrict Nasser's ability to unite Arabs, convinced Nasser to punish the West and exercise his independence by nationalizing the Suez Canal, which he did on July 26, 1956. The Canal was owned and operated by the Suez Canal Company, with stock held largely by British and French investors. Anthony Eden, the British Prime Minister was furious and immediately began looking for a military option to wrest control of the Canal from Nasser. An incident associated with his response is worth telling:

Two days after the nationalization, Eden called Captain Liddell-Hart[33] into his office and ordered him to develop a plan to regain the Canal and force Nasser out of power. Hart developed four plans for Eden, who rejected each in order. The fifth plan Hart presented Eden was exactly what he wanted. It was a duplicate of the first plan and Liddell-Hart told Eden that -- Eden responded by throwing an ink well at Hart to which Hart: "picked up a government issued waste paper basket, and jammed it over the prime minister's head."[34]

---

[32] The Soviets routinely used Warsaw Pact countries as an avenue for arms distribution. Czechoslovakia was particularly active.

[33] Liddel-Hart was a well known British military historian and theorist. One of his key projects was to organize Field Marshal Erwin Rommel's papers and letters, place them in historical context, provide commentary and publish them as the *Rommel Papers* in 1953.

[34] Chris Leininger, "Suez Crisis", http://history.acusd.edu/gen/text/suez.html. Accessed July 22, 2005.

Eden moved forward with an invasion plan, even against Dulles' advice. He agreed to a joint operation with the French and Israelis, an action unthinkable in the Middle East because a military operation conducted in association with Israel would virtually destroy Britain's international leverage in the region.

The actual attack was a coordinated setup. By prior agreement with Britain and France, Israel attacked Egypt on October 29, 1956. Britain and France publicly demanded both sides (Egypt and Israel) stop fighting, or they would land troops – which they did, to secure the Canal. Everyone paying attention saw through the ruse.

The Eisenhower Administration was facing a presidential election, and had condemned the Soviet Union for their heavy-handedness in putting down a revolt in Hungary the same year. President Eisenhower was convinced he could not display a double standard, so he responded quickly and directly to the French and British invasion by demanding their immediate withdrawal. Meanwhile, Nasser shut down the Canal and cut British and French forces off from the oil they needed to continue operations and, as a consequence, became a hero in the Arab world. Britain's ally, Iraq, severed ties and moved into Nasser's camp. Britain's ability to influence the Middle East that had been carefully nurtured over the course of a century was destroyed in a day. The United States was able to increase influence in the Middle East by being seen as opposing Britain, France and Israel. The real winner of the day, however, was the Soviet Union. The Soviet leaders wisely stayed on the sidelines and continued to groom their relationship with Nasser in the aftermath.

## 1967 Arab-Israeli War (Six Day War)

The US and the USSR forced Israel to withdraw from the Egyptian territory seized during their 1956 campaign. During the following years, tensions between Arab states and Israel continued, and Arab East-West alignment generally falling out with Egypt and Syria looking to the USSR and Jordan to the West. Throughout the decade leading up to the 1967 war, Syria raided and harassed Israel. In 1967, Syria and Egypt signed an agreement to aid each other militarily. Israel responded to Syrian raids and artillery attacks with reprisals. In May, Nasser (still in charge in Egypt) demanded that Israel stop responding, and planned to place military forces into the Sinai, which was then occupied by UN peacekeepers. He also blockaded Israeli ports to strangle Israel economically. Internal pressures in Jordan convinced Jordan's King Hussein that he needed to come to a military agreement with Egypt, so he signed a mutual defense treaty with Nasser on May 30, 1967. Jordan's entry into the escalating crisis changed the strategic situation for Israel. Jordan occupied the west bank of the Jordan river, and was only 17 miles from the Mediterranean Sea – presenting Jordan with a prime opportunity to attack and split Israel in two. This threat, coupled with Egyptian aggressiveness, a hostile Ba'athist[35] regime in Syria, and the United States encouraging caution, convinced Israeli leadership that they must strike first or risk extinction. Nasser knew that his actions would cause Israel to attack first – and that was his intent. With his control of Syrian and Jordanian armed forces, he felt that an Israeli first strike would damage their standing in world opinion and would be militarily disastrous for them. Nasser's "basic objective will be the destruction of Israel. The Arab people want to fight".[36]

Israeli Prime Minister Abba Eban went to the United States on May 26, 1967 to talk with the Johnson Administration about applying pressure to Egypt to prevent a war. Upon his arrival,

---

[35] The "Arab Socialist Ba'ath Party" is a secular pan-Arab organization founded in 1945 by an Orthodox Christian, Michel Aflaq. Originating in Syria, Aflaq combined romanticism, Arab nationalism and socialism in opposition to the French (and other Western European influences). Over time the party fragmented into Marxist and conservative factions. Ba'athism has been strongest in Syria (where it is the controlling party) and Iraq (where it ran the country from 1968 to 2003).

[36] President Nasser, "On This Day", *BBC*, http://news.bbc.co.uk/onthisday/hi/dates/stories/may/30/newsid_2493000/2493177.stm. Accessed July 26, 2005.

Eban received intelligence that the Egyptians were going to attack within 48 hours, and he requested immediate assistance from President Johnson. This was a time when the war in Vietnam was escalating, and President Johnson wished to maintain focus on his Great Society initiative at home – he didn't need a crisis in the Middle East. Using the "hot line", Johnson contacted Soviet Premier Alexis Kosygin and suggested that if the USSR wished to avoid a global crisis, they should inform the Egyptians to back off. The Soviets moved quickly and Nasser backed down. The Israeli leadership, convinced that neither the US nor the UN would come to their assistance, decided on a preemptive strike. Israel attacked Egypt on June 5.

Israel's first military priority was to destroy the Egyptian Air Force to gain air superiority for the support of ground forces. The air attacks quickly took out the Egyptian Air Force, giving the Israeli Air Force a free hand over Egyptian territory. The Israeli army then defeated the Egyptians in the Sinai. In the central part of the country, the Jordanians attacked into Israel around Jerusalem but were stopped and pushed back so that the Israeli's captured the West Wall and Temple Mount area previously controlled by Jordan. On the West Bank, Israeli forces defeated the Jordanians and seized territory on the west side of the Jordan River. In the north, along the Golan Heights where Syrian artillery had been raining shells down on Israeli villages, the Israeli's hesitated. The Israeli Air Force had destroyed approximately 2/3rds of the Syrian Air Force, but military planners predicted that a fight to take the Golan Heights would be very costly. The Israelis did attack on June 9, and by June 10, they held the Golan Heights.

On June 11, when a cease fire was signed, Israel occupied the Sinai, the Gaza Strip, the West Bank (including East Jerusalem), and the Golan Heights. In the aftermath, over 300,000 Palestinian Arabs fled to Jordan where they threatened to destabilize the Jordanian government.

President Nasser claimed that the United States and Britain provided direct combat support to the Israelis with aircraft flown from aircraft carriers. This charge, picked up by the Arab press, affected the Arab view of the US in years to come. Both the US and British governments strenuously denied direct combat roles in the war. Another impact of the war was the creation of the "Palestinian problem" with Israeli occupation of the Gaza Strip and the West Bank, fomenting unrest among Palestinian Arabs for decades to come.

## 1973 Arab Israeli War (Yom Kippur War)

After the 1967 war, Israel began building fortifications in the Sinai and along the Golan Heights. President Nasser died in 1970 and was replaced by Anwar Sadat, who along with Syria's president Hafiz al-Assad, intended to recapture their lost territories. Sadat began a military buildup and undertook measures to correct the deficiencies uncovered during the 1967 war, particularly in Egyptian air defense capabilities. Sadat also faced a deepening economic crisis, and felt that a military victory would provide the groundswell of support necessary for him to push through needed, but unpopular, domestic reforms. His way to national stability was through recovering lost national pride. In Syria, Assad focused on building the largest and best equipped Arab army, one he felt could recapture the Golan Heights from Israel.

In 1970, King Hussein of Jordan faced an internal crisis when a war ("Black September") broke out between the Palestine Liberation Organization (PLO) and the Jordanian government. The PLO began wearing uniforms, carrying arms and acting as police within the Palestinian camps in Jordan. The PLO created a state within a state. After Jordan and Egypt agreed to the "Rogers Plan" proposed by the United States for a cease fire between Egypt and Israel and an Israeli withdrawal from the occupied territories, the PLO decided to undermine the pro-Western Jordanian government. Black September started with a PLO attempt to assassinate King Hussein, which failed. Syria intervened on the side of the PLO. Ultimately, Jordan prevailed in this war, and the Palestinian militants were driven into Lebanon.

In 1972, Sadat openly stated that he intended to go to war with Israel. He thoroughly modernized his armed forces with the latest Soviet equipment. The Russians were a mixed blessing for Sadat, however. The Soviets, attempting to avoid another confrontation like 1967, agreed with the United States to maintain the "status quo" in the region. This was at a time when the Soviets and the Nixon Administration were attempting to achieve a degree of stabilization in the Cold War – "*détente*", as engineered by Henry Kissinger, Nixon's Secretary of State. The Soviets also began leaking details of Egyptian preparations for the war, so Sadat expelled Russians from Egypt in 1972 (after he got the equipment he wanted).

Although warned by several sources of an impending attack (including a secret flight by King Hussein to talk with Golda Meier, Prime Minister of Israel), the Israeli leadership decided not to conduct a preemptive attack. They were not convinced a war was eminent, and they knew they could not count on direct American support if they went to war first.

When it came, the Egyptian attack on Israeli lines in the Sinai ("Bar Lev Line") was very effective. Well rehearsed, planned and coordinated, the Egyptian Army quickly overwhelmed most of the Israeli fortresses. The front line Egyptian units were exceptionally well equipped with anti-tank weapons, and operated under an effective air defense cover that defeated the Israeli Air Force. Ultimately, the Israelis were able to infiltrate, then surround Egyptian units by crossing the Suez Canal using bridging equipment that was made from materials purchased from French scrap yards. In the north, along the Golan Heights, Syrians used the same tactics as the Egyptians (heavy anti-tank capability with an effective air defense cover). The Syrians achieved some initial success, but were eventually stopped as Israeli reservists strengthened, and then held the line. Beginning October 11, 1973, Israeli forces pushed into Syria far enough to shell the outskirts of Damascus. King Hussein of Jordan entered the war by sending forces to aid the Syrians in successfully stemming the Israeli tide.

The United Nations, led by the US and USSR, negotiated a cease fire agreement to take effect on October 22. Egyptian and then Israeli units violated the agreement, and in the process, the Egyptian Third Army was cut off by the Israelis. Kissinger, recognizing that the situation gave the US leverage over the Soviets and the possibility of permanently removing Egypt from their sphere of influence, pushed the Israelis not to destroy the Egyptian Third Army. In the meantime, Leonid Brezhnev, the Soviet Premier, sent a note to President Nixon threatening that if the US would not act in concert with the USSR to stop the fighting, that the Soviet Union would enter the war on the side of the Egyptians. Henry Kissinger convened an emergency meeting of key Administration leaders (Nixon did not participate because of preoccupation with the Watergate scandal). Kissinger sent a bland response to the Russians, sent a note to Sadat telling him to stop asking for Soviet help, and convinced Secretary of Defense James Schlesinger to raise the defense condition level (DEFCON) to the highest peacetime alert level. The Soviets detected the increase in the American alert level and concluded that the US was willing to go to war over the issue (problems with ending the war in Vietnam aside). They backed down on their demands. In the end, the Israelis agreed to direct negotiations with Egypt. Kissinger brokered an agreement and United Nations peacekeepers were placed in the Sinai between the two forces.

The United States became brokers for peace as a result of this war. Ultimately, the *Camp David Accords*, organized by President Jimmy Carter in 1978, stabilized relations between Egypt and Israel, resulted in the return of the Sinai to Egyptian control, and excluded the USSR from the process. Within the mid-East, Arabs states concluded that they could not attack Israel directly and win – so terrorism became a viable option for many organizations and some states, such as Syria and Libya. As for Egypt's position in the Arab world – Egypt was seen as a traitor for negotiating and concluding a peace with Israel, and was expelled from the Arab League. Anwar Sadat was assassinated in October 1981 by members of the Egyptian Army.

Another outcome of the war was the 1973 oil crisis. Before the war even ended, Arab members of the Organization for Petroleum Exporting Countries (OPEC) met and agreed to restrict oil access to nations that supported Israel during the war – including the United States and countries of Western Europe. Although the war triggered this action, the OPEC countries also intended to increase the value of their natural resources by driving up the price of oil. The action included an embargo on oil to the US and the Netherlands. The Middle Eastern oil exporting countries gained economic freedom as a result of this action – and realized a way to force the West to go in directions they wished. The embargo ended in March 1974, but the effects of the crisis made an already shaky American economy even worse for the remainder of the 1970's.

## *The Iranian Crisis - 1979*

In 1953, the CIA supported a coup that returned Shah Mohammad Reza Pahlavi to power in Iran. The Shah had fled Iran when the socialist, anti-Western Prime Minister, Dr. Mohammed Mossadegh, dissolved Parliament and assumed dictatorial powers. British Intelligence, along with the CIA's Kermit Roosevelt,[37] assisted in overthrowing Mossadegh and returning the young Shah to Iran. During the next several years,

---

[37] Kermit "Kim" Roosevelt, Jr. was the grandson of Theodore Roosevelt and distant cousin to Franklin. He was an OSS officer during World War II in the Middle East and taught at Harvard after the war, until he was recruited for the CIA in 1950. Critics of the coup contend that Mossadegh would have liberalized Iran, without American intervention, if left in place. Roosevelt later contended that Mossadegh's rule would have led to a take-over by the Iranian communist party, and thus subjugation by the Soviet Union.

the United States maintained a close relationship with the Shah's government, providing economic and military assistance in exchange for a guaranteed supply of oil. Iran also acted as a friendly counter to the Soviet Union, who shared their northern border. The Shah's government was corrupt and repressive, particularly against radical Muslim activists. The Shah's opponents, however, also included the Iranian middle class that was not benefiting from oil profits flowing into the country. In response to growing criticism, the Shah began a series of reforms that ran counter to a growing Muslim fundamentalist movement within the Muslim world in general and within Iran in particular. These reforms included: abolition of the feudal system (which deprived some Muslim clerics of their income), suffrage for women (which was strongly opposed by the Muslim clerics), attempts to minimize the role of Islam on Iranian daily life and his refusal to ban alcohol, movies and tobacco. In 1963, in response to the Shah's reforming efforts, Ayatollah Khomeini issued a *fatwa* (a religious edict) against the Shah's reforms. The Shah responded by cracking down on dissidents, using soldiers and his secret police (SAVAK). Khomeini was arrested, which led to anti-government riots, government killing of demonstrators and more arrests. Khomeini was exiled, but remained the center of anti-government activity for years to come. Although the Shah's modernizing efforts continued and the economy expanded during the 1960's and 1970's, many Iranians remembered his 1963 crackdown.

When Jimmy Carter became president in 1977, he attempted to shift American international relations policy from containment of communism to human rights. Accordingly, his Administration suggested to the Shah that if human rights conditions did not improve in Iran, the nation would face a cut in support. The Shah complied and as he lessened repression, a burgeoning revolution expanded and violence escalated on both sides. In January 1978, the official government-backed newspaper ran a story critical of Khomeini, demonstrations ensued and the Iranian army was sent in to crack down on the demonstrators. Several students were killed and the mourning period was used by clerics in mosques around the country as an opportunity for more protest, and more were killed – with this cycle repeating itself over and over. Damage and protests ravaged the economy, and in the summer of 1978, the government was forced to employ austerity measures, causing more unrest among the general population. Consequently, the working class joined students, clerics and intellectuals in anti-Shah protests. The Shah began to give in to demands by Muslim clerics to crack down on Western influences, but riots and demonstrations continued. Meanwhile, in Paris, Khomeini became a celebrity. With members of the international press flocking to his door, Khomeini gave four or five interviews a day. By November 1978, the Shah was losing support among his military. In December, protests became even more violent.

Groups opposing the Shah were diverse and included intellectuals, communists, political liberals and Islamic radicals – and they all believed they could use Khomeini to achieve their ends. The liberals among them believed they could push Khomeini aside after the Shah was deposed and establish a democracy. Khomeini had other ideas.

The Shah's last attempt to stave off the inevitable was to announce a new constitution and a new Prime Minister – Shapour Bakhtiar. As the situation deteriorated, Bakhtiar recommended to the Shah that he leave the country. The Shah and his wife fled to Egypt on January 16, while their three children went to the United States. Bahktiar then allowed Khomeini to return to Iran on February 1, 1979. On February 11, students seized government buildings and a radio station, along with arms and ammunition. Beginning in March, Khomeini began issuing orders establishing Islamic law as the basis for Iranian law, and reversing the Shah's reforms. He announced that corruption would be punished by death, newspapers were banned, political groups (including those that had opposed the Shah) were banned, and the United States was characterized as the "Great Satan".

In dealing with Iran, President Jimmy Carter was faced with two options. He could support the Shah's use of power to suppress growing opposition to his rule, or he could support protest groups to smooth the transition to a new Iranian post-Shah government.[38] He did neither – instead he encouraged the Shah to back off repressive tactics, then allowed history to run its course. Regarding Carters actions (or inaction), Gaddis Smith said, "President Carter inherited an impossible situation – and he and his advisors made the worst of it."[39] Critics accused Carter of "losing" Iran, much as critics blamed Truman for "losing" China thirty years earlier. However, the consequences of losing Iran included exportation of radical Islamic anti-American terrorist organizations, funded, equipped and trained by Iran. Through the 1990's, Iranian backed terrorists operated not only in the Middle East, but were extremely active in Europe (in places such as Bosnia that has a large Muslim population) and allied themselves with like-minded anti-American terrorist organizations, such as Al Qaeda.

After leaving Iran, the Shah lived in Egypt, the Bahamas and Mexico. Suffering from lymphatic cancer, the Shah sought treatment in the United States, but President Carter was reluctant to allow him to enter the country. Eventually, he relented, and allowed the Shah to come to the United States for treatment in October 1979. When considering the Shah's request, Carter asked his advisors for their recommendations. Most recommended allowing the Shah into the United States. Carter's rejoinder was "And if (the Iranians) take our employees in our embassy hostage, then what would be your advice?" Vice-President Mondale reports that no would could answer his prescient question.[40] The Shah died in Egypt on July 27, 1980.

---

[38] "Jimmy Carter: People and Events, The Iranian Hostage Crisis", *PBS* www.pbs.org/wgbh/amex/carter/peopleevents/e_hostage.html. Accessed August 3, 2005.
[39] Ibid.
[40] Ibid.

In response to the Shah's visit to the US, Khomeini urged Iranians to demonstrate against the US on November 1, 1979. On November 4, a large crowd of students gathered outside the US embassy in Tehran and seized the embassy building. Sixty-six hostages were taken. Similar actions occurred elsewhere in the region. For example, Libyan dictator Muamar Qadhafi ordered a mob to attack the American embassy in Tripoli on December 2, 1979.[41]

President Carter groped for a solution to the crisis. His presidency, whose crowning achievement was the *Camp David Accords*, was mired in economic troubles, an inability to work with Congress (even though it was controlled by his own party), and charges that he had given away the Panama Canal. Carter attempted negotiations to release the hostages, but Khomeini demanded a return of the Shah to face trial. Meanwhile, the President authorized a poorly organized and coordinated rescue mission, attempted the night of April 24-25, 1980. Controlled directly from the White House, the mission turned into a disaster. Secretary of State Cyrus Vance resigned in the aftermath – he had opposed the mission. Ultimately, the hostages were returned to the United States after 444 days of captivity on Ronald Reagan's inauguration day in 1981. Although planned, no further rescue missions were attempted. President Carter's inability to deal with crisis, the economy and Congress left a legacy of perceived ineptitude.

The Iranian Crisis displayed apparent American impotence in the face of a determined, but weaker force. Regimes, terrorists and the Soviet Union took note. This, in the aftermath of Vietnam, framed a perception that the US could be dealt with effectively through terrorism and coercion. For Iran, the crisis and its aftermath placed them in the forefront of anti-American terrorism for decades.

---

[41] Ironically, President Carter's brother Billy was hired by Qadhafi to lobby the United States on behalf of Libya in 1980.

# Lebanon - 1983

Internal instability stemming from the struggle for control of the Lebanese government between Muslims and Christians came to a head in the 1970's. After independence from France during World War II, Maronite Christians maintained a majority in the country and controlled the Lebanese government. However, an influx of Muslims (including Palestinians after the various Arab-Israeli conflicts) eventually resulted in the creation of a Sunni Muslim majority. Pressure from Muslims and leftists, working against Maronite control of the government resulted in political factions establishing armed militias. These militias were supported by outsiders: Maronites by West Germany and Belgium; Sunnis by Iraq and Libya; and Arab socialists and Palestinian organizations (the PLO and the Democratic Front for the Liberation of Palestine) were supported by the Soviet Union.

After Black September in Jordan, Yasser Arafat moved his headquarters to Lebanon (along with Soviet financing and logistics support). Muslims in southern Lebanon welcomed the PLO as a counterweight to the Maronites and allowed the PLO to establish a safe haven there to carve out a "state within a state" and launch attacks on Israel.

Conflict broke out in 1975. In January 1976, a Syrian backed Palestinian militia attacked Damour, a predominantly Christian city. The Palestinians' rampage of rape, mutilation and murder resulted in at least 582 deaths. This incident convinced Christians that the Palestinians had to go and responded with violence. As the fighting spun out of control, the Lebanese government asked Syria to help stabilize the situation. Syria entered Lebanon and a Christian militia responded by massacring 2,000 Palestinians at Tel al Zaater.

In March 1978, Arafat's PLO Fatah militia seized a bus in Israel, resulting in a confrontation that left 34 Israelis and six terrorists dead. Israel invaded Lebanon four days later. Although the Israelis withdrew under UN pressure, they retained

45

control of portions of southern Lebanon to protect their borders. A cease fire agreement between Israel and the PLO did little to stop PLO bombings and rocket attacks, and Israeli retaliation. Abu Nidal, who had split with Arafat in 1974, attempted to assassinate the Israeli ambassador in London in June 1982. After an Israeli retaliation against the PLO and a PLO rocket and artillery attack into Israel, the Israelis again invaded Lebanon. The Israelis drove the PLO into Beirut then laid siege to the city. A cease fire was negotiated by American diplomat Philip Habib that included an Israeli pullback from the city and withdrawal of the PLO. These actions were to be overseen by peacekeepers that included US Marines as well as French and Italian units. While peacekeepers were untangling warring factions around Beirut, the Israelis, in concert with a Lebanese militia group, looked for PLO members hiding in Palestinian refugee camps. That hunt resulted in the massacre of 700-800 Palestinians between September 16 and September 18, 1982. During a subsequent investigation by the Israeli government, Defense Minister Ariel Sharon was held responsible for actions that led to the massacre, and he was forced to resign from his post.

On April 1983, a suicide bomber struck the US Embassy in West Beirut killing 63 then on October 23, 1983, a truck bomb hit the US Marine barracks and a French barracks that killed 241 American and 58 French servicemen – establishing the multinational peacekeeping force in Lebanon as a terrorist target. Responsibility for all attacks is generally attributed to *Hezbollah*, which was supported by Iran and Syria.

With the commitment of US Marines to peacekeeping, the United States changed from the role established in the 1950's as a distant peace broker to an immediate target of various anti-American factions operating in Lebanon. The French attacked Iranian Revolutionary Guard positions in the Bekaa Valley of Lebanon following the US Marine and French barracks bombing. The US planned, but cancelled a similar attack on Iranian Revolutionary Guard positions. The Marines were moved aboard ship to prevent a repeat of the attack on their barracks, and in 1984, the peacekeeping force was removed. The war in Lebanon sputtered on for years.

The Reagan Administration's non-response to the Marine barracks attack further reinforced the idea that the US could be targeted with little or no punishment in return. The idea that the US could be attacked without retribution most certainly emboldened terrorist organizations in the Middle East.

## Libya

During the 1970's and 1980's, Muammar al-Qaddafi's Libya actively sought to undermine US influence in the Arab world, and to unite Arab and Third World countries, along with various terrorist organizations against the United States. No discussion of the era would be complete without mentioning Qaddafi's role in making several US presidents' lives miserable.

Qaddafi, a young Libyan army officer, led a coup against the pro-Western King Idris in 1969. Inspired by Nasser in neighboring Egypt, Qaddafi melded socialism, pan-Arabism and pan-Islamism into regime that became a haven to terrorist organizations such as the PLO. Qaddafi developed ties with the Soviet Union, who supplied his military with advanced weapons, including the MIG-25 aircraft – one of the most advanced fighters in the world at that time. Over time using funds generated from oil, Qaddafi financially backed several terrorist acts. Among attacks that Western governments claimed he supported were the Black September organization's attack of Israeli athletes at the 1972 Munich Olympics, the 1986 bombing of a Berlin discothèque that killed three and wounded over 200, attacks by Palestinian terrorists on crowds at the Rome and Vienna airports, and the destruction of Pam Am Flight 103 over Lockerbie, Scotland in 1988. Additionally, Qaddafi reportedly paid international terrorist "Carlos the Jackal" to kidnap Saudi and Iranian government officials.

After Ronald Reagan became president in 1981, the FBI identified a Libyan as a suspect in a murder in Chicago. Reagan closed the Libyan embassy and began seeking opportunities to reduce Qaddafi's influence in the region. Reagan concluded that Qaddafi was attempting to establish "a single nation of fundamentalists under rigid religious control".[42] He met with Egyptian president Sadat and discussed Qaddafi's involvement in terrorist acts in general, and his attempts to destabilize governments in the region. At that time, the Defense Department was planning military exercises in the Gulf of Sidra, international waters north of Libya that Qaddafi claimed as Libyan territorial waters. Reagan planned to send a message to Qaddafi that the United States was not intimidated by him. Sadat expressed satisfaction with this plan, describing it as "magnificent".[43]

In August 1981, Libyan aircraft approached the US carrier taskforce in the Gulf of Sidra, 60 miles north of Libya. Two US F-14's intercepted and destroyed two Libyan aircraft. Then, after the Berlin disco bombing in April 1986, Reagan ordered a bombing raid into Libya. The raid, conducted on April 14 against selected targets around Tripoli and Benghazi, resulted in the deaths of 60 people (including Qaddafi's adopted daughter). After the Pan Am Flight 103 disaster, the UN imposed sanctions on Libya. The Pan Am bombing seemed to be a turning point for Qaddafi. He found himself diplomatically isolated, without Soviet support (after the USSR dissolved), enduring UN sanctions and with diminishing income from oil exports. On top of that, his army tried to assassinate him in 1993 and protest riots developed in 1996 after a soccer game. Qaddafi began working to improve relations with the West. His condemnation of the September 11, 2001 attacks was the most forceful of any Arab leader. In 2002, Qaddafi offered to pay $2.7 billion in compensation to victims of the Pan Am attack. Apparently

---

[42] Ronald Regan, "National Defense – Libya", http://www.ronaldreagan.com/libya.html. Accessed September 26, 2005.
[43] Ibid.

impressed by American removal of Saddam in 2003, he announced that Libya possessed weapons of mass destruction programs, and that he intended to dismantle them with international assistance.

## *Conclusion*

US involvement in the Middle East took shape after World War II. With the decline of British influence and the rising appreciation of American power and economic prowess in the midst of the Suez Crisis in 1956, America's role and prestige increased dramatically. American foreign policy in dealing with Arab nationalism of Nasser and Sadat was relatively effective. However, the ability for the United States to deal with radical Islam, beginning with the Iranian Hostage Crisis and going through the "War on Terror" was severely challenged. The Carter Administration's reaction to Iran – negotiation based on past understandings of how the Middle East worked – failed miserably. A new age dawned with the Iranian Revolution, and Islamic fundamentalism replaced secular political attempts to unify Arab nations (note that the Iranians are not an Arabic people, they are of Persian descent) with a focus on brotherhood rather than political unity. America's support of Israel, always an issue, became the centerpiece of Islamic hatred of the United States. Finally, during this period, the means of conflict changed from conventional military activities to terrorism, and from symmetrical to asymmetrical application of military power.

# Chapter Three

# The US, Central America and the 1980's

*"We must not break faith with those who are risking their lives . . . on every continent from Afghanistan to Nicaragua . . . to defy Soviet aggression and secure rights which have been ours from birth. Support for freedom fighters is self-defense."*

Ronald Reagan
1985 State of the Union Address

American's involvement in Central America during the 1980's revolved around President Ronald Reagan's commitment to roll back communist gains made at the expense of US security during previous administrations. During President Carter's watch, the communists acquired Grenada and Nicaragua. When Carter attempted a secret dialogue with Fidel Castro, the communist dictator of Cuba, to address issues of human rights violations in the region, Castro reported to the Soviet Ambassador to Cuba that Carter's approach to him revealed America's weakness and the fact that the US was reeling from a series of "crippling defeats suffered by American imperialism in the Western Hemisphere", specifically the loss of Grenada and Cuba.[44] To others, Castro said he enjoyed toying with President Carter – talking with him about human rights while at the same time supporting anti-American insurgencies.

With Fidel Castro's rise to power in Cuba, the ability for the Soviets to export communism to other parts of Latin America was realized. Castro supported the creation of the Sandinista National Liberation Front (*Frente Sandinista de Liberacion Nacional* - FSLN) in 1961 to oppose the corrupt Somoza

---

[44] Conversation from Soviet archives as reported by Peter Schweizer, *Reagan's War: The Epic Story of His Forty-Year Struggle and Final Triumph over Communism.* (New York: Doubleday, 2002), 104.

50

family's decade's long control of Nicaragua. Unsuccessful in raising support during the 1960's the organization become more successful during the 1970's as the increasingly politicized peasants were evangelized by socialist clerics preaching liberation theology. A critical turning point in the movement came with an earthquake in 1972. The Somoza regime pocketed money donated by the international community for their own use instead of rebuilding Managua, the capital of Nicaragua. Hardly less savory than the dictator they sought to overthrow, the FSLN, led by KGB "trusted agent" Carlos Amador established a special action group located on the US-Mexico border to strike targets in the United States on behalf of the KGB. This effort included targeting American diplomats. On December 27, 1974, the FSLN attempted to kidnap American Ambassador to Nicaragua, Turner Shelton, at a dinner party. They missed Shelton, but managed to kill the former Nicaraguan Minister of Agriculture, Jose Maria Chema Castillo and hold a number of people hostage. The Somoza government negotiated with the FSLN for $1,000,000 and a plane ride to Cuba. The assassination attempt had been sanctioned by Castro (according to KGB files). In 1979, President Carter called for Somoza's removal, and cut off aid to Nicaragua. A FSLN led uprising forced Somoza to flee the country. He was eventually assassinated in Paraguay. The Sandinistas assumed control of Nicaragua. At the time, President Carter said that the revolution was not Cuban influenced, but an opportunity for the people of Nicaragua to choose a government.[45]

## *Impact of Liberation Theology*

The impact of liberation theology in creating popular support for the Sandinista regime was critical to their initial success. This "theology", preached among the severely underprivileged of Latin America and urban North America, was an applied philosophy, drawing inspiration from European humanism, socialism, progressive evolution and Marxism. Taking shape in

---

[45] Ibid., 110.

the early 1960's, liberation theology was ultimately defined by Gustavo Gutierrez, a Catholic theologian, in his *Teologia de la liberacion*, published in 1971.

The essence of Gutierrez' thesis is described by D. D. Webster in the *Elwell Evangelical Dictionary*:

> Liberation theology accepts the two-pronged "challenge of the Enlightenment". These two critical elements shape liberation theology's biblical hermeneutic. The first challenge comes through the philosophical perspective begun by Immanuel Kant, which argued for the autonomy of human reason. Theology is no longer worked out in response to God's self-disclosure through the divine-human authorship of the Bible. This revelation from "outside" is replaced by the revelation of God found in the matrix of human interaction with history. The second challenge comes through the political perspective founded by Karl Marx, which argues that man's wholeness can be realized only through overcoming the alienating political and economic structures of society. The role of Marxism in liberation theology must be honestly understood. Some critics have implied that liberation theology and Marxism are indistinguishable, but this is not completely accurate.
>
> Liberation theologians agree with Marx's famous statement "Hitherto philosophers have explained the world; our task is to change it". They argue that theologians are not meant to be theoreticians but practitioners engaged in the struggle to bring about society's transformation.[46]

Liberation theology, primarily a Catholic enterprise, was refined in a series of meetings in the 1960's held in Mexico, Columbia, Cuba, Montreal and Peru. Liberation theologians started with the idea that orthodox theology is biased against the

---

[46] D. D. Webster, "Liberation Theology: Advanced Information", http://mb-soft.com/believe/txn/liberati.htm Accessed July 27,2005

poor and supports the capitalistic class that exploits them. They believed that their thesis on orthodox Christianity was true within given societies, and also among nations. Sin was seen as a lack of brotherhood among men, capitalists were sinful because they oppress, the oppressed were sinful when they allow the oppression. Salvation was the act of bringing about a new social order where everyone is equal (equivalent to the communist ideal of a classless society). Christ served as an example (not God), and the church was the means whereby the revolution can be achieved. As liberation theologians defined their dogmas and process, they began to integrate their preaching into local parishes using articulate, charismatic preachers who brought a message of earthly salvation to people who were victims of repressive Latin American dictators. It was but a short step to the support of communist insurgencies in Central American countries. The approach was brilliant and the effect dramatic.

## Sandinistas and the Contras

After the Sandinistas assumed control of Nicaragua, the Carter Administration's Deputy Secretary of State Warren Christopher appeared before the Senate to request aid for the new regime, stating that the new government would be characterized by "popular participation." Carter pushed through a $75 million package for the Sandinistas,[47] who were also receiving help from the Soviets.

The KGB, recognizing the need to keep their relationship with the Sandinistas covert, issued the following secret communiqué regarding their strategy:

The FSLN is the ruling political organization. The leadership of the FSLN considers it essential to establish a Marxist-Leninist Party on the basis of the front, with the aim of building socialism in Nicaragua. At present, for tactical reasons and in view of the existing political situation in the

---

[47] Schweizer., 110.

Central American region. The leadership of the FSLN prefers to make no public statements about this ultimate goal.[48]

The day after seizing power, East Germany began helping the FSLN set up a secret police operation. Within a year, the KGB was planning to use Nicaragua as a base for shipping weapons, ammunition, uniforms and other supplies to communist insurgencies in surrounding Central American countries.

Opposition to the Sandinistas was almost immediate among native peoples who resisted the socialization process. Generally led by disaffected former members of FSLN (who saw their revolution co-opted into a communist regime) natives objected to: Sandinista efforts to deny natives access to resources in their living areas (so the regime could exploit these resources for industrialization); the arrest and execution of tribal leaders; the destruction of villages; the conscription of young men into the Nicaraguan military; the forced removal of 10,000 Indians from their traditional lands (in moves remarkably similar to Stalin's depopulation activities of the 1930's); and the economic blockades of villages not supportive of the Sandinista regime.[49] A growing number of anti-Sandinista opposition groups became known collectively as the "Contras".

President Carter, recognizing his error in supporting the Sandinistas, began to provide support to the Contras prior to his departure from office, kicking off what was subsequently known as the "Contra War".[50]  In March 1981, newly inaugurated President Reagan authorized CIA and Pentagon support to the Contras. In November 1981, Reagan set aside $19 million for

---

[48] Ibid.
[49] "Contras", http://enlwikipedia.org/wiki/Contras.  Accesseed July 27, 2005
[50] Ronald Hilton, "President Reagan", *World Affairs Report On-Line*. http://wais.stanford.edu/Politics/politics_presidentreagan.htm. Accessed July 28, 2005.

support of Contra activities against the Sandinista regime. However, opposition in Congress grew, with Congressional Members making comparisons between Central America and Vietnam, and accusing the Contras of violating human rights (alleged by a human rights organization – Americas Watch). Congress passed the *Boland Amendment* in 1982 cutting off military support to the Contras. The legislation was extended in 1984 to cover all Federal government agencies. In response, the National Security Council (NSC) worked to raise private and foreign funds in support of the Contra efforts. Beginning with the *Boland Amendment*, Congressional military support to the Contras was very uneven and given grudgingly. However, Congress did better at providing funding for humanitarian support to the Contras.

In addition to supporting the Contras, the Reagan Administration began conducting joint military exercises off the coast of Nicaragua and in neighboring Honduras. The liberal American response to joint military exercises in the region was quick. Governors (including Massachusetts governor Michael Dukakis) refused to allow their National Guard troops to participate, accusing Reagan of attempting to create a war in the region. In Nicaragua, the Sandinistas viewed American support to the Contras and the military exercises with alarm. Leaders in Cuba and the Soviet Union were also concerned with the double threat of a growing Contra insurgency and Americans next door in Honduras (where US ground forces had taken up residence). Castro began to pull advisors out of Nicaragua. Daniel Ortega, the undisputed leader of the Sandinistas, suspended the constitution and freedom of the press and suppressed political dissent.

The US invasion of Grenada in 1983 caused the Soviets to seriously consider the possibility that the US might invade Nicaragua. The East Germans, in particular, were concerned about a threat to their investment in the area. An internal *Stasi* (*Ministerium fuer Staatssicherheit* – East German Ministry for State Security) memorandum of the time reports: "It has been learned from leading circles close to J. (Jesse) Jackson that the Reagan Administration is preparing for a direct armed intervention in Nicaragua."[51]  In the aftermath, Castro went to the Soviets for additional funding, who more than doubled the rate of support to given Cuba compared to what they had given in the previous decade.  Internal Soviet and East German memoranda, available since the fall of the Soviet Union indicate that Reagan's strong anti-communist policies in the region were causing Castro and his Soviet allies to reconsider the gains they had made at the expense of the United States during the previous decade.  Ultimately, in 1989, Mikhail Gorbachev, then leader of the failing Soviet Union, sent a message to Daniel Ortega that the FSLN could no longer expect Soviet support due to financial difficulties.  The next year, in free elections, Ortega went down in defeat.

During the 1980's, liberal critics of President Reagan worked to circumvent his Administration's efforts to defeat the Sandinistas.  Reagan's support of the Contras was widely attacked by liberal politicians and the press.  Senators John Kerry and Tom Harkin's visit to Nicaragua in 1985 is a case in point.  Kerry and Harkin met with Ortega, who said that he would moderate his policies and not allow the Soviets to establish bases in Nicaragua.  A few days later, as Kerry urged Congress to disapprove military funding to the Contras, Ortega flew to Moscow to ink a $200 million deal with the Russians. The mainstream press seemed to side with the American liberals and reported stories favorable to the Sandinistas.  For example, Peter Collins, a former *ABC News* correspondent reported that the late *ABC* evening anchor, Peter Jennings, rejected his draft report on the 10th anniversary of the Sandinista regime in 1989 and called him on the phone to dictate to Collins what to say on the air.  Asked why he thought Jennings would do this, Collins responded, "Because I presume that Peter Jennings felt that the Sandinista regime, which was a communist regime – no question

---

[51] *Stasi* memorandum of September 24, 1984: *John O. Koehler Collection*, Hoover Institution Archives, Stanford University.

56

about it – were mere benign agrarian reformers . . . (Jennings) was a believer, was and is."[52]    Even decades later, when President George W. Bush nominated John Negroponte[53] to be the new national intelligence director, the *Washington Post's* basic assumption that his role in the Contra War was controversial and therefore a reason to question his fitness to serve in that position.[54]    Media coverage also tended to emphasize human rights abuses by the Contras and neighboring US friendly Honduras, but not the Sandinista government.

Human rights abuses were present on all sides during the conflict.    The Sandinistas relocated 8500 Miskitos (native peoples) from their land to create free fire zones.    The Sandinista led Nicaraguan Army killed and imprisoned leaders of several native peoples and conducted at least two massacres of Miskito's in 1981 and 1982, including aerial bombardment of villages, shooting of prisoners, burning villages and confiscated livestock. Indians fled across the border to Honduras for protection.[55] Contras were also accused of human rights abuses by various organizations including Americas Watch.    In neighboring Honduras, death squads reportedly killed 184 political activists during the 1980's.

---

[52] Marc Morano, "Whistleblower Denounces ABC's Marxist Bias, CNN's Propaganda for Saddam", *CNSNews.com*, May 1, 2003.   As reported    at    www.newsmax.com/achives/articles/2003/5/1/160050. shtml, Accessed October 23, 2005.

[53] John Negroponte was the US Ambassador to Honduras from 1981-1985.   Critics alleged he covered up Honduran death squad activities. He was involved in channeling funds to the Contras, an activity that grew into the Iran-Contra scandal.

[54] Michael Dobbs, "Negroponte's Time in Honduras at Issue", *Washington Post*, March 21, 2005.

[55] "Report on the Situation of Human Rights of a Segment of the Nicaraguan    Population    of    Miskito    Origin",    Inter-American Commission on Human Rights, Organization of American States. November 29, 1983.

# Iran-Contra

In the aftermath of the *Boland Amendment* and subsequent Congressional blocks of US government military aid to the Contras, the NSC sought private and third country funding. In June 1985, the Israelis approached the Reagan Administration with a proposal. The Israelis offered to act as an intermediary in the sale of arms to Iran in exchange for freeing of American hostages held by Iranian backed militias in Lebanon. Secretary of State George Shultz and Secretary of Defense Casper Weinberger both opposed this idea. However, President Reagan, after meeting with the families of hostages, considered and rejected their advice; he was intent on freeing the hostages. At the time, Iran was engaged in a deadly war with Iraq, and needed military assistance. As a bonus, funds generated from the sale of weapons would be used to support the Contras. Initially, arms were provided through Israel, but in 1986, an individual intermediary was used. Unfortunately, *Hezbollah*, an Iranian backed group, took more additional hostages than were released, so the "arms for hostage" program was cancelled. However, the sale of arms to Iran continued until the operation was revealed by a Lebanese magazine *Ash-Shiraa* in November 1986. A Congressional investigation and a commission appointed by President Reagan both concluded that members of the Administration were guilty of several crimes, and that the President failed to properly supervise his subordinates. The scandal was a major blow to the Administration and their support of the Contras, and was memorable due to US Marine Lieutenant Colonel Ollie North's congressional testimony.

# El Salvador

While the war in Nicaragua raged, the *Farabundo Martí National Liberation Front* (FMLN) a Marxist confederation, conducted a war against the government of El Salvador.

In 1972, a reform minded El Salvadoran presidential candidate and leader of the Christian Democratic Party (PDC),

Jose Napoleon Duarte, was defeated in an election widely considered to be fraudulent. Duarte was exiled and widespread discontent grew throughout the country. Intending to capitalize on this discontent, leftists groups began an armed insurrection against the government in 1979. In October 1979, military officers and civilians rebelled and overthrew the government. Duarte joined the revolutionaries and led the provisional government until March 1982, when new elections were scheduled. The interim government began to take steps to reform the country, but internal divisions grew. The FMLN continued an insurgency on the left, while the extreme right saw Duarte's reforms as too liberal (thus, in their minds, pro-Marxist) and began a reign of terror characterized by death squads that targeted leaders of the PDC as well as the FMLN. Perhaps the most notable death squad assassination was the killing of the popular Archbishop Oscar Romero in 1980.

In 1983, Salvadorans elected a new assembly and a provisional president was selected by that assembly. In 1984, Duarte won the first free election held in the country in 50 years. His opponent was Roberto D'Aubuisson, whose party had close ties to the death squads and, it was rumored, had ordered the death or Archbishop Romero. The CIA supported Duarte's election with approximately two million dollars. Later, in 1989, Alfredo Cristiani won the presidential election, and when he took office, it signified the first time a peacefully elected civilian leader took over from another peacefully elected civilian leader. In El Salvador's case, democratic processes didn't immediately stop the violence. Death squads and the FMLN continued to operate.

Attempts by President Cristiani to negotiate a peace in Mexico City in September 1989 ended in failure, and were followed by a deadly offensive on the city of San Salvador by the FMLN, in which hundreds of people were killed. The army responded by stepping up counterinsurgency activities. A death squad composed of government soldiers (later convicted) killed six Jesuit priests – leading to international outrage and the cutoff of US aid to the government.

Subsequently, the UN Secretary General became involved in negotiations that resulted in a peaceful settlement of differences and demobilization of the FMLN.

During the war, the United States, and in particular, the Reagan Administration was blamed by critics for supporting activities of the death squads. These claims gained credibility when two graduates of the US Army's "School of the Americas"[56] were allegedly involved in Archbishop Romero's assassination. Generally, reports of FMLN murders were marginalized or blamed on the government while right wing death squad murders were widely reported (as in the case of the Jesuit priests) by the American press. The US supported Duarte and Cristiani (both freely elected presidents) in their attempts to deal with the death squads while at the same time trying to defeat the communist insurgency. With the FMLN's support structure undercut in neighboring parts of Central America and the Caribbean, the Marxist rebels were essentially forced to negotiate for an end of hostilities. When possible, murderers on both sides were tried and convicted. Many were later released as part of a general amnesty program.

## *Grenada – Operation "Urgent Fury"*

On March 13, 1979, Maurice Bishop seized power in a bloodless coup on the Caribbean island of Grenada. Bishop was leader of the "New Joint Endeavor for Welfare, Education and Liberation" movement (also known as "New Jewel"). He was a

---

[56] "School of the Americas" (SOA) attracted attention from the press and critics of American involvement in Central America during the 1980's. SOA was designed to provide a professional military education to Latin American officers by the US Army. A number of graduates were later involved in human rights abuses, so the school became derisively known as "School of Assassins". Twenty-three of the 27 soldiers involved in the 1989 killing of six Jesuit priests (noted in the text) were graduates of SOA.

Marxist and a close friend of Fidel Castro. According to East German documents, after Bishop's seizure of power, Castro told Erich Honaker (the East German head of state), "For thirty years, we have been isolated, on our own, now there are already three of us in the region: Grenada, Nicaragua, and Cuba. Grenada has important implications in the Caribbean, where there is instability after the success of revolution in Nicaragua." The KGB quickly began to provide arms and ammunition to Bishop's new government.

Bishop began building a large international airport on Grenada with Cuban assistance. The Reagan Administration publicly stated that the airport was designed to support military operations – which would provide Cuba and the Soviets an excellent location to range the Caribbean with land based aircraft. Bishop denied the charges (after the war, documents discovered supported the Administration's claim). In addition, intelligence indicated that Grenada was a transit point for infiltrating communist rebels into El Salvador.

Bernard Coard, the hard-core Marxist Minister of Defense, initiated a coup and arrested Bishop in October 1983. Coard had Bishop shot, declared martial law and instituted a curfew. The Organization of Eastern Caribbean States (OECS) requested US assistance in dealing with the aftermath of the coup – but the request itself was apparently issued at the behest of the United States.

Over the objections of the British government (Grenada was within the British Commonwealth), the United States invaded Grenada on October 25, 1983. The Reagan Administration's stated reason was to protect 600 American medical students on the island and to secure the airfield. Operation "Urgent Fury" was completed by November 3, with all military objectives (including rescuing the students) achieved. Seven thousand American troops were joined by 300 personnel from Antigua, Barbados, Dominica, Jamaica, Saint Lucia and Saint Vincent. They encountered 1,200 Grenadian soldiers, 784 Cubans (636 of which the Cuban government claimed were constructions workers – but were armed and had military training), 49 Soviets, 24 North Koreans, 16 East Germans, 14 Bulgarians and 3 or 4 Libyans.

Troops were withdrawn by mid-December and a new government installed. The Governor General named an advisory council that administered the country until general elections were held in December 1984. The country's constitution, which had been suspended by Bishop's government in 1979, was restored. The American invasion proved popular among the island's population due to Coard's execution of Bishop and imposition of the curfew and martial law. US troops were hailed as liberators. The American students were glad to see them too.

Cuban and Soviet confidence was shaken in the aftermath of the US invasion. Reagan's efforts to roll back communist advancement were bearing tangible fruit. For the first time a country that had been communist was no longer communist. In a top secret Soviet Central Committee study on Ronald Reagan, researchers concluded:

> Although the immediate target of the policy of 'neoglobalism' (the "Reagan Doctrine") now is mainly countries of the Third World, above all those with progressive regimes, its spear point is directed in practice against the Soviet Union and socialism as a whole. . . (His real objective) was not only to stop the further spread and consolidation of positions of socialism in the world, but also to 'exhaust' the USSR and its allies . . . wearing it down in conflicts in different regions of the world.

## *Panama – Operation "Just Cause"*

The final act of US resolve in Central America during the 1980's was an invasion of Panama. By the time the Panamanian crisis came to a head, President Reagan had left office, replaced by his former Vice President, George H. W. Bush.

Critics claimed that the invasion, originally named Operation "Blue Spoon", was invented to reverse an agreement to hand over the Panama Canal to Panama, and to reestablish military bases in the area. The charge that the US intended to go back on the commitment made by President Carter in the *Torrijos-Carter Treaties* was made more tenable by fact that Panamanian President Manuel Noriega intended to appoint a close ally to administer the Canal. These charges ignored the underlying nature of the Noriega regime and his growing ties with communist nations (Nicaragua and Cuba).

Panama came into existence because of the Canal. President Theodore Roosevelt (who was President from 1901 to 1909) was committed to building a canal across a portion of Central America to reduce travel distance for the US fleet and commercial ships around the south end of South America. Late in the 19th century, the United States was beginning to realize a naval revolution proposed by American naval officer and philosopher Alfred Thayer Mahan, and to apply principles of sea control necessary for successful warfare and commerce. Building a canal in Central America was not a new idea – the French had already attempted to build one. When a treaty negotiated by the US with Columbia for $10 million down and an annual fee of $250,000 for rights to build a canal was rejected by the Columbian government (they wanted more money and objected to American sovereignty of the Canal Zone), Roosevelt encouraged the leadership of the French owned New Panama Canal Company to organize a rebellion in Panama (at that time, Panama was part of Columbia). When Columbian troops landed on the isthmus to put down the rebellion, the American owned railroad running across Panama refused to transport them. US Navy presence offshore also served to intimidate the Columbian government. American support ensured success of the revolution, and President Roosevelt's Secretary of State quickly recognized the new nation and inked a deal with the new Panamanian government to obtain access to the Canal Zone (a 10 mile strip along the present Canal) – on the same terms as originally attempted with Columbia. The 52 mile project was completed in 1914 – an engineering marvel of the time.

The Panama Canal provided income and strategic security to the United States for the next several decades and two world wars. Over time, nationalists in Panama began to resent American control of their prime economic asset and began to agitate to take over operation of the Canal. President Carter signed agreements known as the *Torrijos-Carter Treaties* in September 1977, which were ratified by the Senate (by one vote) in April 1978. The treaties stated that the Panama Canal would be turned over to Panama by December 31, 1999 (with the US reserving the right to defend the Canal) and that the Canal would be neutral territory open to vessels of all nations.

Brigadier General Omar Torrijos, the Panamanian dictator who signed the Canal treaties with President Carter, died in a plane crash in 1981 and was succeeded by an intelligence officer, Manuel Noriega. Once Noriega took control, he worked both sides of the street by cultivating friendships in the US intelligence community and the Medellin drug cartel in Columbia. In 1985, President Reagan's National Security Advisor John Poindexter and Elliot Abrams, Assistant Secretary of State for Inter-American Affairs, warned Noriega that the US was concerned about his monopoly on power and dealing in the Columbian drug trade.

In June 1987, a former chief of staff in the Panamanian Defense Force (PDF) accused Noriega of involvement in Torrijos' death (Noriega later claimed that the US Government killed Torrijos), of election fraud and the murder of his prime political opponent, Hugo Spadafora, in 1985.[57] This revelation further strained relations between the US and Noriega and caused demonstrations in Panama. The United States Senate passed a resolution asking Noriega to leave office. Anti-

---

[57] Ronald H. Cole, *Operation Just Cause*. (Washington DC: Joint History Office, Office of Chairman Joint Chiefs of Staff, 1995), 6.

American mobs stormed the US embassy, resulting in State Department action to stop aid to Panama. Federal grand juries in Miami and Tampa indicted Noeriega on drug trafficking charges on February 5, 1988. Noriega began a campaign of harassment of US citizens following his drug indictment. Deprived of US aid, he sought economic assistance from Cuba, Nicaragua (thus Soviet) and Libya beginning in 1988. Communist block countries funneled weapons into Panama with Nicaraguan assistance. Noriega created a militia of "Dignity Battalions" (a private army), trained with communist block expertise. Libya provided $20 million to Noriega in return for using Panama as a base for training Central American based terrorists for use throughout Latin America. Noriega's links with Nicaragua, Libya and Cuba are consistently underplayed or ignored by standard texts dealing with the Panamanian invasion.

After indictments were filed by the grand jury, the US Joint Chiefs of Staff began planning military action against Noriega. In May 1989, an anti-Noriega coalition supported candidates that were elected to president and vice president. On May 10, Noriega blamed foreign interference for the election results (even though his Dignity Battalions attempted voter intimidation) and nullified the elections results. Opposition leaders were physically attacked and went into hiding. On October 3, 1989, Panamanian military leaders attempted, and failed, to lead a coup against Noriega. They were tortured and shot.

As tensions between the US and Noriega escalated, the US began infiltrating troops into Panama and began seriously planning for military operations. On Friday, December 15, 1989, the Panamanian General Assembly, controlled by Noriega, passed a resolution stating that a state of war existed between Panama and the United States. The next day, four US officers in a civilian car took a wrong turn and ran into a PDF checkpoint (critics later echoed Noriega claims that they were conducting a reconnaissance operation). Shots were fired at the unarmed US officers who fled but ran into another checkpoint and a hail of gunfire. Three officers were wounded, one died. In the meantime, a US naval officer and his wife who observed the incident were detained and taken to a police station. Panamanian interrogators beat the officer and assaulted his wife.

Operation "Just Cause" began at 0100 hours, December 20, 1989. (See Figure 2) Shortly after the start of the operation, President Bush identified four reasons for attacking Panama: first, to safeguard American lives; second, to defend democracy and human rights; third, to combat drug trafficking; and fourth to protect the integrity of the *Torrijos-Carter Treaties*.

Panamanian forces were quickly subdued by multiple simultaneous operations. Within hours of the invasion, Guillermo Endara, winner of the presidential elections earlier in the year, was sworn in as president. Noriega was elusive, but with a one million dollar reward on his head, he decided to seek refuge at the Vatican diplomatic mission in Panama City. In a famously televised operation, US forces played loud rock music outside the residence. Noriega finally surrendered to US forces on January 3, 1990. He was immediately taken to the US for processing and trial based on outstanding warrants from the drug indictments.

Twenty-three Americans were killed and 324 wounded. Panamanian military casualties numbered 314. Civilian casualty estimates range from 200 (US Southern Command) to 2,000 (Ramsey Clark, in a private, politically motivated "Commission of Inquiry") to a more realistic estimate from the Physicians for Human Rights of about 300.

US forces assisted in establishing a new government, but widespread looting had a long-term negative impact on the Panamanian economy. After US withdrawal, Panama concluded a series of successful elections, in which opposition candidates won and were able to assume office unhindered. President Clinton fulfilled US promises of the *Torrijos-Carter Treaties* in turning over the Panama Canal on December 31, 1999, although concerns were subsequently raised about contracts to operate the Canal being given to Hutchison Whampoa, a Hong Kong based company owned by Li Ka-shing, who US intelligence believes has strong ties to the communist Chinese People's Liberation Army.

## *Conclusion*

Ronald Reagan was widely vilified in the media and by his political opponents for the US intervention in the affairs of Central America. However, in 1988, the Sandinistas were eventually coerced into a cease fire (brokered by Costa Rica), and into free elections in 1990. Beginning in 1990, successive free, democratic elections were held in Nicaragua, with the Sandinistas consistently losing. Democracy – though shaky, descended on a nation ruled for decades by dictators of the right and left. And what about the Contras and Sandinistas? They are now political entities participating in a viable democracy. Grenada was the first communist nation to become non-communist, and to move to a democracy. Panama, edging toward communism through the opportunistic policies of Manuel Noriega was pulled back from the brink – and democracy established with a pattern of free and fair elections. Ultimately, El Salvador moved from a cycle of Marxist and right wing violence to a viable, though troubled, democracy.

The Soviets and the Cubans, at first gratified at the expansion of communism in the region, reached a fever pitch of despair after the fall of Grenada. Ironically, as the Soviet Central Committee reports indicate, the Soviets understood Reagan's agenda much more clearly than many politicians and most of the press in the United States. And they were rightly concerned.

A footnote to the Contra War is the CIA's possible involvement in moving drugs into the United States as a means to fund the Contras. A series of articles written by Gary Webb entitled *Dark Alliance* details the alleged drug operations. Subsequently, investigators have obtained declassified documents that both support and refute Webb's allegations – but this story has taken on the aura of an urban myth in its retelling and resonated with many that opposed American involvement in Central America.

## Chapter Four

# Winning the Cold War

*"Here's my strategy on the Cold War: We win, they lose."*
Ronald Reagan

George Kennan, a young diplomat stationed at the American Embassy in Moscow at the end of World War II knew that his government was in trouble. The Truman Administration, like a child lost in the woods, was aimlessly attempting to make sense of a drastically changed world. Much like events 45 years later (with the fall of the Soviet Union), the strategic paradigm had shifted. Enemies – Germany, Japan and Italy – were subdued and would soon become good friends. Allies – Russians, British and French – would change as well. The Soviet Union was becoming a competitor and perhaps an enemy of the US. Britain, weakened by two world wars and the depression, was no longer the power she once was. France was desperately attempting to regain its previous colonial glory – but would fail in the next decade. Sitting in his office in Moscow, Kennan (who died in 2005 at the age of 101) penned a document that provided strategic clarity for more than 45 years – his famed "Long Telegram".

Immediately following World War II, President Truman assumed that the Soviets and Americans would continue their friendly relationship, but the US immediately encountered "push back" from the Russians. In February 1946, after the Soviet rejection of the World Bank, the US Embassy in Moscow received a request from Washington for some insight, based on their experience, about why the Soviet's made such a decision. Kennan responded with his "Long Telegram", in which he laid out the following conclusions regarding the Soviet Union:

- The Soviet Union saw itself encircled by capitalist powers, which required waging a relentless battle against capitalist interests and leaders.
- The basic Russian view of the world is neurotic which drives Soviet policy and propaganda.
- Soviets will take every opportunity to advance their own power and weaken their enemy's. They will take opportunities in Third World countries to extend their influence.
- Expect that communist activity around the world will be coordinated through Soviet influence. They will attempt to use international organizations, the Russian Orthodox Church, and nationalistic movements to undermine Western influence.
- The way to counter the Soviet threat is by containing them within their current borders. Kennan's recommendation became known as the policy of "containment".

Kennan's telegram included a well known and poorly understood (in terms of practical application) statement; "if Soviet power was impervious to the logic of reason" it was "highly sensitive to the logic of force."

Long after Kennan sent his telegram to Washington, during a speech given at the Polish United Workers Party (the Polish Communist Party) in November 1968, Soviet Premier Leonid Brezhnev annunciated the "Brezhnev Doctrine". He said, "When forces that are hostile to socialism try to turn the development of some socialist country towards capitalism, it becomes not only a problem of the country concerned, but a common problem and concern of all socialist countries." The practical implication of this statement was that no country – once under communist control, would be allowed to become free.

The Soviets, as we have already seen, focused on involvement in the Third World to achieve the gradual domination of the communist system – the Warsaw Pact[58] countries, communist China, North Korea, Southeast Asia, Cuba and Nicaragua – and influence in other regions, particularly the Middle East and Africa. They did have their share of early defeats. They failed to establish a communist regime in Greece after World War II (due primarily to President Truman's application of containment) and in Italy and France, because the Marshal Plan in took the heart out of communist attempts to influence the majority in those nations.

To some extent, every President from Truman to Carter subscribed to the concept of containment. It was applied in Greece, Korea and Southeast Asia. After the US pullout in Vietnam, it was somewhat discredited and replaced (only to an extent) by the concept of *détente*, or engagement, as proposed by the Nixon Secretary of State, Henry Kissinger. President Carter attempted a human rights basis for international relations early in his presidency, but fell back on containment as his policies failed.

## *A "National Malaise"*

In 1977, President Jimmy Carter inherited a country with serious economic problems, and just beginning to recover from the national trauma of the Vietnam War. During the 1976 presidential campaign, Carter promised honesty, in contrast to the popular perception of deceit and corruption resulting from the Watergate scandal and President Fords' pardoning of Richard Nixon in its aftermath. Because he eschewed politics, President Carter had difficulties in getting his programs through Congress, even though it was controlled by his own party. In assessing a

---

[58] The Warsaw Pact was a Soviet led military and political union established in response to the creation of North Atlantic Treaty Organization (NATO). It was composed of the USSR, Albania (who withdrew in 1961 over ideology, then formerly left in 1968), Bulgaria, Romania, Hungary, Poland, Czechoslovakia and East Germany. Yugoslavia's communist dictator, Tito, did not join the pact, remaining officially neutral throughout the Cold War.

second oil crisis in 1979 (the first was in 1973), rising interest rates and inflation, Carter concluded that the United States would no longer be able to expand, but must turn to conservation, implying that the nation's best days had already passed. Carter's approval ratings fell to 26% - below Richard Nixon's lowest ratings during the Watergate crisis. Carter retreated to Camp David, and then gave a television address in which he essentially scolded the American people for allowing themselves to sink into a "national malaise" and a "crisis of confidence". In the area of foreign affairs, Carter was instrumental in brokering the *Camp David Accords*, but failed to understand the true nature of the Soviet Union, and was taken aback by the Soviet invasion of Afghanistan in 1980. His Administration also mishandled the crisis in Iran to the extent that the Iranian hostage taking was also a surprise that immobilized his foreign policy during the last year of his Administration.

By the end of the 1970's, the United States appeared to be in decline. A staggering economy, loss of prestige among allies, loss of ground to the Soviets, and a general feeling of "malaise" pressed down upon the American people. Patriotism ebbed, doubts about the future prevailed. But two events occurred that made 1980 a more promising year.

The first was the 1980 Winter Olympics at Lake Placid, New York. Now known as the "Miracle on Ice", the United States Olympic Hockey Team accomplished something that hadn't been done since 1960 – winning an Olympic gold medal in hockey, and they beat the dominating Soviet team in the process. The Soviet team was a world class professional organization that defeated the National Hockey League (NHL) All Star Team in 1979 by a score of 6-0. In an exhibition match on February 9, just prior to the Olympics, the Soviets easily outclassed the US Olympic Team by a score of 10-3. In short, the Soviets were untouchable. The US team progressed through a series of matches – not perfectly, but good enough to finally meet the undefeated "Red Machine" on February 22, 1980. People around the nation were glued to their television sets in awe as the pickup American hockey team led by coach Herb Brooks managed to defeat the USSR by 4-3. Although the game against the Russians was not the last game of the tournament for the United States, it was certainly the most memorable. The Americans went on to win the gold medal by beating Finland by a score of 4 to 2.

A simple game, but that event helped to restore a sense of national pride and patriotism that melted away in the jungles of Vietnam. The sense was, "We can beat the Russians. They are not ten feet tall after all."

The second event was the election of Ronald Reagan.

## The "Reagan Doctrine"

President Carter had difficulty articulating international and domestic policies. Internationally, he focused initially on human rights as the touchstone of his foreign policy. He assumed that he had the ability to deal with the Soviets with moral equivalency and that they had the same or similar objectives. Ronald Reagan, as president, took a totally different approach to the Soviet Union.

Reagan assumed the Soviets sought communist expansion and to undermine Western democracies.

In July 1978, (Reagan) penned a commentary that completely captured (Premier Leonid) Brezhnev's secret 1969 decision at Yalta to strive for strategic superiority over the United States. . . . In November 1978, he wryly noted that Moscow was concentrating its arms control negotiating strategy on limiting American technological advances while giving itself an advantage in the areas it favored. In doing so he was perfectly describing the secret strategy General (Nikolay) Detinov (Soviet General Staff Officer and arms control expert) was seeking to carry out – namely, using arms control to gain superiority.[59]

On June 8, 1982, President Reagan addressed the British House of Commons.

If history teaches anything, it teaches self-delusion in the face of unpleasant facts is folly. We see around us today the marks of our terrible dilemma--predictions of doomsday, antinuclear demonstrations, an arms race in which the West must, for its own protection, be an unwilling participant. At the same time we see totalitarian forces in the world who seek subversion and conflict around the globe to further their barbarous assault on the human spirit. What, then, is our course? Must civilization perish in a hail of fiery atoms? Must freedom wither in a quiet, deadening accommodation with totalitarian evil?

Reagan recognized the economic nightmare faced by the Soviet Union and underscored that when compared to free nations, the centrally planned communist economic system was consistently less efficient and often left their people destitute. In his Parliament speech he made comparisons between similar nations that had possessed free and communist economies respectively and how they were faring in the world: Malaysia and Vietnam, West Germany and East Germany, Austria and Czechoslovakia. Reagan expressed confidence that the Soviet economic system was failing and would fail. He declared that communism would end up on the ash-heap of history. This remarkable speech was given more than eight years before the fall of the Berlin Wall.

Economic and international professionals disagreed. Columbia University's Seweryn Bialer said, "The Soviet Union is not now nor will it be during the next decade in the throes of a true system crisis for it boasts enormous unused reserves of

---

[59] Schweitzer, 106.

political and social stability that suffice to endure the deepest difficulties." Famous Harvard economist John Kenneth Galbraith said as late as 1984 that, "the Russian system succeeds because, in contrast to the Western industrial economies, it makes full use of its manpower."[60]

In his famous "Evil Empire Speech" delivered to the National Association of Evangelicals on March 8, 1983, Reagan said:

> Yes, let us pray for the salvation of all of those who live in that totalitarian darkness -- pray they will discover the joy of knowing God. But until they do, let us be aware that while they preach the supremacy of the state, declare its omnipotence over individual man, and predict its eventual domination of all peoples on the Earth, they are the focus of evil in the modern world.

And in response, Reagan's critics piled on. A sampling is provided by Timothy Carney in an *American Spectator* article on the passing of Ronald Reagan:

> Back in D.C., *Washington Post* doyenne Mary McGrory called the performance "a marvelous parody of a revivalist minister, flaying those laggards who refuse to join his crusade against the nuclear freeze and the 'evil empire' of the Soviet Union." *Post* peacenik Colman McCarthy called it "a return to a 1981 outburst that the Soviets are liars and cheats. Both preachments lower [Reagan's] thinking to the level of Ayatollah Khomeini..." Historian Henry Steele Commager, already long in the tooth, declared that this was "the worst presidential speech in history, and I've read them all." A news story quoted former Carter speechwriter Hendrik Hertzberg as saying, "Something like the speech to the evangelicals is not presidential." Sister publication *Newsweek* joined the pile on, predicting that the speech

---

[60] Ibid., 143.

would hobble the president's re-election chances.

In Congress, the halls reverberated with Democratic mockery. From the House floor, Rep. Ed Markey summarized Reagan's position thus: "The force of evil is the Soviet Union and they are Darth Vader. We are Luke Skywalker and we are the force of good." Rep. Tom Downey said, "Mr. Speaker, the only thing the President didn't tell us last night was that the evil empire was about to launch the death star against the United States."

And the Speaker, Tip O'Neill, nowadays touted as Reagan's good bipartisan buddy, had his own theological axe to grind. "The evil," he retorted, "is in the White House at the present time, and that evil is a man who has no care and no concern for the working class of America and the future generations of America, and who likes to ride a horse. He's cold. He's mean. He's got ice water for blood."[61]

The reaction in the Soviet Union was a little different. Andrei Zorin was listening to the *BBC World Service*, a forbidden radio station in the Soviet Union, when he heard Ronald Reagan refer to the Soviet Union as the focus of evil, and an evil empire. He was floored. Many people thought it – but the President of the United States actually said it. "The Soviet Union was an absolute evil for democratic society, and Reagan's approach was absolutely correct,"[62] said Lev Pnomaryov, a human rights advocate. Certainly the Soviet government was outraged by his words, but Reagan gave hope in the gulags.

---

[61] Timothy P. Carney, "A Touch of Evil", *American Spectator*, undated.
[62] Susan B. Glasser, "Ambivalence in Former 'Evil Empire'", *Washington Post*, June 7, 2004, page A1.

Putting legs to his view of the Soviet Union, President Regan articulated his "Reagan Doctrine" [63] during his 1985 State of the Union address. In it, he said:

We must stand by all our democratic allies. And we must not break faith with those who are risking their lives—on every continent, from Afghanistan to Nicaragua—to defy Soviet-supported aggression and secure rights which have been ours from birth.

Although Reagan had broken with "containment" in practice, here he made it publicly formal. He adopted John Foster Dulles' "Roll-Back" strategy from the 1950s – the idea that the US would push back against communist advancement, and take back what had been lost, but Reagan intended to do it overtly.

This view was officially promulgated in a *National Security Directive* in 1983, which said:

The U.S. must rebuild the credibility of its commitment to resist Soviet encroachment on U.S. interests and those of its Allies and friends, and to support effectively those Third World states that are willing to resist Soviet pressures or oppose Soviet initiatives hostile to the United States, or are special targets of Soviet policy.

Reagan put this doctrine into practice through support of anti-communist organizations in the Third World – most notably in Nicaragua and Afghanistan.

## *Regan Pressure Points*

The Conventional Force Buildup: Following the Vietnam war, the US Army arguably reached its lowest level in moral and

---

[63] "Reagan Doctrine", US Department of State, http://www.state.gov/r/pa/ho/time/dr/17741.htm. Accessed July 28, 2005

overall military effectiveness during the 20<sup>th</sup> Century. Although large amounts of money had been spent in fighting the war, relatively little of it went into general military readiness and new weapons programs. Following the end of the Vietnam War, General Creighton Abrams identified five key systems that were critical to the successful conduct of the future Army's ground mission – the M-1 (later known as Abrams) tank, the Bradley Fighting Vehicle, the Black Hawk and Apache helicopters and the Patriot Missile System. Other military services had similar acquisition programs – but the cost of the Vietnam War and funding reductions during the early years of the Carter Administration slowed or stopped many programs. Ronald Reagan, convinced that it was necessary to restore American power in order to counter the Soviet military, moved quickly with his military buildup program. In the early 1980's for example, the Soviet Union had 194 active rifle, tank and airborne divisions while the United States had only 16. In 1979, only six of the ten stateside divisions were considered combat ready, while only one of the four US divisions in Europe was combat ready. In 1980, only 50% of soldiers recruited were high school graduates, and in the late 1970's, the quality of soldiers recruited was so low that nearly 40% of them were discharged before the end of their first enlistment for disciplinary or unsuitability reasons.[64]

A revolution in military thought accompanied the new weapons systems and a renewed focus on the military profession within the Services. The failure to rescue the hostages in Iran during the hostage crisis underscored the state of military forces in the minds of many people in the United States. In the early 1980's the US Army produced an updated Field Manual 100-5 to describe the "Air-Land Battle", an operational doctrine designed to dissect and defeat Soviet style land forces. Like the US Hockey Team, American military professionals no longer looked upon the Russians as ten feet tall and invincible. To improve the

---

[64] Robert Scales (Ed), *Certain Victory: The US Army in the Gulf War*, (Washington DC: US Army, 1993) 16.

78

quality of soldiers, General Maxwell Thurman (who was a Major General at the time) refurbished the Army's recruiting command, selecting only the best and brightest as recruiters and hiring Madison Avenue advertising firms to help. The result was the "be all you can be" campaign. The quality of Army recruits improved quickly and dramatically.

Military recovery was necessary for national defense, but Reagan pushed it further. He instituted a staggering $1.5 trillion military buildup, the largest in the nation's history, designed to push the Soviets over the brink in an arms race – a race in which the Russians already had a very big head start.

Intermediate Ballistic Missiles: Between 1977 and 1987, the Soviets deployed 654 SS-20 missiles and 509 launchers. The SS-20 was a mobile intermediate range surface to surface missile system that could deliver three nuclear warheads with each missile. The maximum range of the missile was 3,000 miles, and it was designed to win a nuclear war against the North Atlantic Treaty Organization[65] (NATO) in Europe.

NATO ministers, meeting in Brussels in November 1979 expressed concern at the Soviet deployment of SS-20's and their multiple warhead capability. At that meeting they approved the American deployment of Pershing II missiles to Europe as a counter to the Soviet threat. In the NATO Nuclear Planning

---

[65] NATO was created in 1949 following the Berlin Crisis, a crisis created by the Soviets when they cut off food and fuel to West Berlin from June 1948 to May 1949 in an attempt to starve the western part of the city. West Berlin had become a "bone in the Communist throat" (according to Nikita Khrushchev). West Berlin was occupied by the French, British and US following World War II, and established as a free city under their protection, right in the middle of Communist East Germany. Initial NATO countries included Belgium, Canada, Denmark, France, Iceland, Italy, Luxembourg, Netherlands, Norway, Portugal, the United Kingdom and the United States. Greece, Turkey, Germany and Spain later entered the Alliance during the Cold War. In 1966, France withdrew from the integrated military command, but remained within the Alliance.

Group meeting in Portugal in March 1983, members noted that at that time, the Soviets had deployed 351 operational SS-20 launchers, and counting older SS-4 and SS-5 missiles, they now had a total of 1,053 nuclear warheads in Europe. The ministers confirmed that they wished to move ahead with a dual track strategy of modernizing NATO capabilities (with US nuclear weapons) and arms control negotiations with the Soviets. At that meeting, they agreed with the US proposal that the entire class of intermediate range nuclear force missiles (INF) should be eliminated. Minutes of the meeting also briefly discuss the ongoing flight testing of Pershing II and Ground Launched Cruise Missiles (GLCMs) to be deployed as a counter to the Soviet SS-20s.[66]

Consequently, when the Reagan Administration took office in 1981, plans were already under way to respond to the SS-20 threat. The Pershing II missile was designed to counter the SS-20, with a range of 1,100 miles, a range that could not reach Moscow from Western Europe. The GLCM range was 1,400 miles but took one to two hours from notification to launch. Both systems were clearly designed to be defensive in nature – but possessed the ability to retaliate. This capability was deliberately chosen to demonstrate a no-first strike stance to the Soviets.

Negotiations to limit intermediate range ballistic missiles began in November 1981 in Geneva. The US proposed a "global zero" that would eliminate the intermediate range nuclear force and constrain shorter range missiles. The Soviets rejected the proposal. The Soviets wished to establish a ceiling of deployed warheads that would include British and French warheads, thus eliminate US missiles from the continent of Europe. The famous "Walk in the Woods" Agreement[67] between the negotiators was

---

[66] NATO Nuclear Planning Group Minutes, March 22 and 23, 1983.
[67] The "Walk in the Woods" Agreement was an informal proposal put together by US and Soviet negotiators during a country outing near Geneva in 1982. Essentially, the negotiators agreed to equal levels of intermediate range missile launchers in Europe (75 apiece); no

reached in the summer of 1982, but the Soviets rejected their negotiators' recommendation. At the beginning of negotiations, the Soviets assumed that Reagan's commitment to rearmament was an empty threat and merely a negotiating ploy. The speed and breadth of the rearmament process however, stunned them, as well as the fact that deployment of Pershing II and GLCMs to Europe was supported by NATO nations. The Soviets had been unopposed in this class of weapons until the first US systems arrived in 1983. The Soviet delegation walked out of negotiations in Geneva with the arrival of the new American weapons systems.

1985 was a turning point for INF negotiations and US-Soviet relations. The Soviet politburo realized that they were losing momentum in the Cold War. Ilya Zaslavsky, a member of the Soviet Congress of People's Deputies "later said that the true originator of *perestroika* (restructuring) and *glasnost* (openness) was not Mikhail Gorbachev but Ronald Reagan."[68] Suspended talks resumed in January 1985. Over the next two years, a series of meetings between negotiators, as well as Reagan and the new Soviet General Secretary Mikhail Gorbachev, result in an agreement on the elimination of intermediate range nuclear missiles as a class. Destruction protocols were agreed in 1987 (ratified by the US Senate in 1988) and missile elimination began in 1988.

During the time that negotiations took place, and in particular during the US deployment of Pershing II and GLCMs to Europe, a highly visible "nuclear freeze" movement gained media attention in Europe and the United States. The stated goal of the various groups that made up the "nuclear freeze movement" was the freezing of nuclear weapons, an objective

---

deployment of Pershing II missiles to Europe and a limit of 90 SS-20 deployments to the Asian part of the Soviet Union (information from the Federation of American Scientists (FAS) website, http://www.fas.org. Accessed October 20, 2005).
[68] Dinesh D'Souza, "How the East Was Won: Why Ronald Reagan Won the Cold War", *American History Magazine*, October 2003.

that would give the Soviets every advantage in the late 1970's and early 1980's when there was no US counter to Soviet intermediate range missiles. In the end, a freeze did not happen – nuclear arms reduction did happen. Interestingly, the freeze movement takes credit for INF and other related arms reduction treaties since. The freeze movement even claimed credit for forcing Reagan to negotiate with Gorbachev.[69]

Strategic Defense Initiative. On March 23, 1983, President Reagan announced the Strategic Defense Initiative (SDI), a system designed to defeat (and make obsolete) Soviet Intercontinental Ballistic Missiles (ICBMs) by employing space and ground based defensive capabilities to destroy ICBMs in flight. Dubbed "Star Wars" by critic Dr. Carol Rosen, advocates gladly adopted the nickname to underscore the fact that today's science fiction is tomorrow's science fact. The program went through several iterations and was made unnecessary in its original scope due to the fall of the Soviet Union. The proposal was designed to aid in hastening the end of the Soviet Union by employing a "strategy of technology" – the idea that technologically advanced nations can take "asymmetric advantage in technology to create and deploy weapons of sufficient power and numbers so as to overawe or beggar its opponents."[70] This "strategy of technology" comes from a book written by Stefan Possony and Jerry Pournelle[71] that was required reading for military officers during the latter half of the Cold War, so the concept was well understood by many American strategists. The Soviet response to Reagan's announcement was alarm. Soviet Foreign Minister Andre Gromyko, in declassified Soviet documents, records his part of a conversation that he had with Secretary of State George Schultz in Geneva:

[69] Lawrence S. Wittner, "Reagan and Nuclear Disarmament", *Boston Review*, April/May 2000.
[70] "Strategy of Technology", *Wikipedia*, http://en.wikipedia.org. Accessed July 29, 2005.
[71] Stefan Possony and Jerry Pournelle, *Strategy of Technology* (Cambridge: University of Cambridge Press, 1970).

If the U.S. did have such a defensive system in place, it would have the capability to inflict a first nuclear strike against the USSR with impunity. One needs no special gift of perspicacity to understand this; it is clear almost to the point of being primitive. If the Secretary were to view this situation from atop the tower, he would reach the same conclusion. The U.S. wants to gain advantage over the Soviet Union, and the defensive system if developed would be used to bring pressure on the Soviet Union. Let us not mince words, even if they are harsh ones: the system would be used to blackmail the USSR."[72]

In 1999, I attended a meeting in Washington DC at which Lady Margaret Thatcher was present. In discussing background to "Star Wars" she said that after Mikhail Gorbachev had become the Soviet General Secretary, he called her and asked if she could speak to President Reagan about backing away from SDI. Lady Thatcher said, "There is a very useful word in the English language that I used that day. I told him 'no.'"

Thatcher, Gorbachev and Reagan all knew what was at stake – the future existence of the Soviet Union. SDI helped bring it to an end, and served its purpose long before the first material fruits of the project were realized.

## Other Critical Influences

The Pope and Solidarity. Pope John Paul II, as Karol Wojtyla, a young Polish man and priest, endured Nazi occupation during World War II which was followed by a repressive communist regime. As a priest, he faced down communist leaders, for example, forcing them to build a church in a so called "workers paradise", the town of Nowa Huta that the government constructed without a church (it was a workers' paradise, and in such a perfect, atheistic place, no church was

---

[72] Schweizer, 244.

needed). Elected pope in 1978, John Paul II returned to his native Poland in an unprecedented visit in June 1979. This visit became a watershed event in the 20th Century.

> In those forty-some sermons, addresses, lectures, and impromptu remarks, the Pope told his fellow-countrymen, in so many words: "You are not who they say you are. Let me remind you who you are." By restoring to the Polish people their authentic history and culture; John Paul created a revolution of conscience that, fourteen months later, produced the nonviolent Solidarity resistance movement. . . And by restoring to his people a form of freedom and fearlessness that communism could not reach, John Paul II set in motion the human dynamics that eventually led, over a decade, to what we now know as the Revolution of 1989.[73]

"Solidarity" was a broad anti-communist movement that began in Poland in 1980. The movement, remarkably, thrived in the Soviet block, where similar attempts had been ruthlessly suppressed (Hungary, Poland and Czechoslovakia). Solidarity began among workers in the Gdansk shipyard and survived because of a growing economic crisis and falling morale, associated with a general weakening of the Communist Party. The movement spread throughout Poland to encompass nine million members. The Polish government attempted crackdowns and outlawed the organization in 1982. Solidarity went underground, supported by the Catholic Church and the CIA. During this time, the Reagan Administration worked with the Vatican and the American Federation of Labor and Congress of Industrial Organizations (AFL-CIO) to help keep the movement alive. In particular, the National Endowment for Democracy, created by Reagan at the suggestion of Georgetown professor Allen Weinstein, assisted by providing direct support to Polish political prisoners and their families, published books and materials that were smuggled into Poland, as well as funding

---

[73] George Weigel, "Pope John Paul II and the Dynamics of History", *Watch on the West,* (Foreign Policy Research Institute), April 2000.

several underground publications within Poland and other Soviet block countries. By 1988, the political and economic crisis in Poland had grown to such an extent that the government was forced to open a dialogue with Solidarity. By the next year, elections were held in Poland, and impact of the movement began to spread throughout Eastern Europe.

The impact of the pope, a visible and effective anti-communist leader, combined with the energy of Solidarity and seeming incompetence of the communist state was synergistically wedded to Reagan's push-back against communism early in his presidency.

Margaret Thatcher. The Prime Minister of England was another factor and important ally at the end of the Cold War. Elected to Tory party leadership in 1975 and as Prime Minister in 1979, her work at home mirrored many conservative initiatives in the United States. Essentially, she focused on rolling back the socialist state that had adversely affected British economic growth the previous decade. In foreign affairs, Thatcher was Reagan's closest ally, supporting his initiatives to defeat communism, allowing the US to base nuclear weapons on British soil and lending support within NATO. As indicated earlier, she understood and underwrote Reagan's philosophy in dealing with the Soviet Union. Perhaps the greatest exception to her partnership with Reagan was the British government's objection to the US invasion of Grenada – which, although it was under Marxist control, remained a member of the British Commonwealth.

Mikhail Gorbachev. Born to a peasant family near Stavropol, he studied law and agriculture and rapidly advanced within the Soviet Communist Party. Gorbachev became a member of the Central Party Committee in 1971 at the age of 40 and the Politburo in 1979, where he worked closely Yuri Andropov, head of the KGB. When Andropov became General Secretary of the Party, Gorbachev supported him and labored to replace much of the Soviet leadership with younger men (friendly to Gorbachev). Upon Andropov's death in 1984, Gorbachev served the new party leader, Konstantin Chernenko, as his second secretary. After Chernenko's short stint and death, Gorbachev was made General Secretary on March 11, 1985 at the age of 54, becoming the first Communist Party leader born after the 1917 Russian Revolution. Gorbachev's selection as General Secretary, according to Georgy Shakhnazarov, one of his foreign policy advisors, was the result of "internal domestic pressures and Reagan's rigid position and that of his administration."[74] Gorbachev offered reforms to recover lost Soviet glory.

Gorbachev initiated three policies designed to free the Communist Party from stagnation: *glasnost*, *perestroika*, and *uskorenie* (acceleration of economic development). Gorbachev supporters in the West later claimed that these policies were designed to help deconstruct the Soviet Union, however Gorbachev was a patriot and intended that his policies would help rebuild a disintegrating Soviet block. But over time, "openness" led to increasing contact with the West and dissatisfaction among repressed populations. Writers, artists and intellectuals, with Gorbachev's permission, began to speak freely and helped to create more open internal freedom and convey Western values and ideas. Gorbachev's restructuring efforts gradually led to the loosening of Soviet control of the Warsaw Pact. Economic acceleration led to invitations to foreign firms to operate within the Soviet Union to help stimulate the Soviet economy.

A major internal crisis with international implications occurred in April 1986, when staff incompetence or negligence resulted in the Chernobyl nuclear power plant disaster. High levels of radiation were released into the atmosphere with global implications. In full view of the world, Soviet mismanagement and rigid counter-productive central control were on display. A sense of decline was evident.

---

[74] Schweizer, 245.

Internal economic crisis, brought on in part by Soviet attempts to match Reagan's arms race, forced radical military restructuring. Gorbachev pulled the Soviet army out of Afghanistan in 1988, admitting the 1979 invasion was a mistake. He withdrew Soviet support from insurgent activities in the Third World, withdrew the Soviet Army from Eastern Europe, permitted the dissolution of the Warsaw Pact and began demobilizing the Red Army in 1988, largely due to the lack of funding. The circle of Soviet influence rapidly diminished with each decision – Gorbachev valiantly fought a losing battle.

In 1991, Gorbachev proposed a new treaty among Soviet republics that would create a truly voluntary federation. Old line communists were still powerful, however, and staged a coup in August to remove Gorbachev from power. Freed after three days of house arrest by the coup plotters, Gorbachev found he was no longer able to control a disintegrating Communist Party. Boris Yeltzin, who defied the leaders of the coup and made a stirring speech on live television from atop a tank, became the hero of the hour. Gorbachev resigned as Executive President of the Soviet Union on December 25, 1991.

Over time, Gorbachev's popularity at home diminished. Many in the Soviet Union knew the downward slide was irreversible and blamed Gorbachev for their national decline. In the West however, Gorbachev was popular and credited by many with ending the Cold War. For example the following statement is found in a standard Western Civilization text, "At summit meetings – with President Reagan and later with President George Bush – Gorbachev successfully pressed for strategic arms reduction."[75] However, Reagan had pushed the Soviets for arms <u>elimination</u> (not just reduction) since 1981. To his credit, Gorbachev did suggest, then agree to significant arms reduction with a view to reduce force structure, save money and help

---

[75] William Perry. *Western Civilization: A Brief History (Fourth Edition)*, (New York: Houghton-Mifflin, 2001), 643.

ensure effective control of weapons in a rapidly deteriorating environment. But Reagan's consistent and unrelenting international weapons elimination policies pushed Gorbachev to the point of concession. In addition, the US provided technical assistance in destroying Soviet weapons that could have disappeared into the murky world of international terrorism.

Soviets in Afghanistan. Another factor that led to the demise of the Soviet Union and end of the Cold War was one of the Soviet leadership's own making. Often identified as the Soviet's Vietnam, their invasion of Afghanistan would have far reaching consequences for decades to come.

The Soviet backed Communist Party in Afghanistan seized control of the government in April 1978 with a coup and established the Democratic Republic of Afghanistan. Retribution on the former ruling elite was immediate. As many as 11,000 people may have been executed with many more fleeing, including 100,000 of Afghanistan's economically critical middle class. The new regime established a Soviet style government, but had difficulty in dealing with periodic uprisings. On February 15, 1979, Adolph Dubs, the US Ambassador was abducted, then killed when the government attempted to rescue him. The US did not send a new ambassador.

In March 1979, the communist Afghan government requested military assistance from the Soviet Union. Limited military support and food aid were promised. Afghans that fled to Pakistan and Iran began to organize themselves into a loose resistance movement.

A split between the two leaders of the Afghan Communist Party resulted in the assassination of one (a poet by the name of Mohammed Taraki) and final domination of the party by the other (Hafizullah Amin). In the aftermath of Amin's seizure of power in September 1979, the Soviets ironically concluded that Amin's brand of Marxism was too radical for a religiously conservative county like Afghanistan, and his rule would only make things worse. An internal Soviet commission, charged with reviewing the situation in Afghanistan, concluded that Amin was purging pro-Soviet members of the party and seeking contacts with Pakistan and China.

The Soviets invaded on December 24, 1979. Amin was killed in the fight and Babrak Karmal, an exiled communist leader was brought back and made the new head of government.

Soviet motivation for invading Afghanistan is difficult to ascertain but contributing factors certainly included the continuing Soviet attempts to ensure a buffer of states around their border. Another issue was the growing Islamic fundamentalism in neighboring Iran and its potential impact on the southern Soviet Republics, composed predominantly of Muslims. Then there was the "Brezhnev Doctrine" – the concept that the USSR had the right to come to the aid of a fellow communist nation, and that Afghanistan was in crisis and needed to be stabilized.

President Carter responded to the Soviet invasion during his January 1980 State of the Union Address. The previous year, Carter had terminated aid to Pakistan because of its developing nuclear program – now he reversed himself and offered a military aid package in exchange for assisting the US in providing support to the *mujahedin* (the anti-Soviet Afghan rebels) and called Pakistan a nation on the front line in the global struggle against communism. Pakistan initially refused aid, but later accepted an offer from Reagan. Aid to fight the Russians in Afghanistan also came from communist China, Egypt and Saudi Arabia.

The Soviets intended for the Afghan army to pacify the countryside, and to only provide support. However, the Russians were drawn deeper into direct combat and the *mujahedin* were effectively supplied and supported – primarily by the CIA and Saudi Arabia – particularly with the deployment of Stinger missiles which essentially denied Soviets effective use of combat aircraft. Tactics used by Soviet and Afghan forces in dealing with the *mujahedin* were brutal. Rural areas were devastated by bombing, forced removal, destruction of livestock and poisoning of water supplies in order to reduce support to the *mujahedin*.

By 1987, Gorbachev faced a dilemma. He had called the war in Afghanistan a "bleeding wound" in his February 1986 Communist Party Congress speech but faced stiff opposition to the withdrawal from the military leadership who had not intention of abandoning the war. Ultimately, internal economic and political problems, growing anti-war sentiment, and Cold War realities led Gorbachev to order a withdrawal. After international jockeying regarding a settlement brokered by the United Nations, the last Soviet troops left Afghanistan on February 15, 1989. The Soviet departure did not lead to peace. The Afghan communist regime, largely ignored by the world succumbed to internal strife in April 1992 and the nation eventually came under Taliban domination.

The cost of the war was extensive. Approximately 15,000 Soviet soldiers were killed and 37,000 wounded. More than one million Afghans died and about five million became refugees. More than five million land mines littered the country by the time of the Soviet withdrawal. The Soviets lost international prestige, ultimately another client state, and billions of dollars consumed by the war.

## Berlin Wall Speech

On June 12, 1987, Ronald Reagan stood before a crowd in front of the Berlin Wall and delivered a speech that, along with Winston Churchill's "Battle of Britain" speech and Franklin Roosevelt's "Day of Infamy" speech, has become a 20th Century classic.

The West German government originally intended for Reagan to deliver a speech to a small crowd in front of the old Reichstag building blocks away, but it was Reagan that insisted on speaking in front of the Berlin Wall. Once a draft of the speech began circulation for comment within the Administration, both the State Department and NSC objected to the language. At one point, Colin Powell (then the Deputy National Security Advisor) specifically met with the speechwriter, Peter Robinson, to insist the language be moderated. Later Secretary of State George Schultz and Senator James Baker also met with Robinson in his boss' office to object. Objections included, "the speech is naïve", "it raises false hopes", "it's clumsy", and is "needlessly provocative". Both the State Department and the NSC submitted their own drafts – according to Robinson, he received a total of seven alternative speeches – none of them included a call for the Soviets to tear down the Berlin Wall.[76]

Administration officials weren't the only ones nervous about what Reagan might say. *Stasi* chief Erich Milke said in a secret directive, "We must count on provocative and slanderous abuse of the DDR" (German Democratic Republic). He directed the *Stasi* to be on "the highest amount of vigilance."[77] The East German government faced several challenges in this speech – not only would it be broadcast live in Germany and later printed, people in East Berlin would be able to hear the speech live on their side of the Wall.

As he gave his speech, Reagan reminded his listeners about freedom and uttered the now famous line, "Mr. Gorbachev, tear down this wall." Although the speech was delivered in English, the crowd erupted immediately

In Moscow, state controlled political commentators called Reagan's speech a rerun of Cold War rhetoric.

Prior to Reagan's speech, arms negotiations with Gorbachev had stalled. After the speech, in December 1987, the two men

---

[76] Peter Robinson, "'Tear Down This Wall': The Inside Story of Reagan's Berlin Challenge", *American History Magazine*, October 2003.
[77] Schweizer, 270.

signed the historic INF treaty eliminating an entire class of nuclear weapons.

## *The End*

1989 has become known as the "year of liberation". The communist government in Poland legalized Solidarity and free elections were held. Hungary abolished their communist government in May and by year's end had established a two party system (neither of which was communist). Events in East Germany were cataclysmic. East Germans began escaping to West Germany through newly opened Hungarian and Czech borders. Protests appeared in the streets, growing to over one million demonstrators in the streets of East Berlin by November 6. The communist government resigned. On November 9, the Wall between East and West Berlin was assailed by tens of thousands of people on both sides. East Germans walked into West Berlin freely. Bulgaria joined the march, but the communist dictator Ceausecu in Romania stubbornly held to the reins of his government, ordering soldiers to shoot demonstrators. Eventually, the army turned on him, and on December 25, 1989, Ceausecu and his wife were tried and executed. Czechoslovakian communist leaders resigned on November 24 and Vaclav Havel, an author, was made president on December 25. Albania – the last of the Soviet block to fall, finally held free elections in February 1991. Yugoslavia, which was communist but had remained neutral during most of the Cold War, also decided to move toward a multi-party system in January 1990.

In the Soviet Union, the government was breaking down and internal forces were attempting to drive the old regime in different directions – democratic reforms or recovery of the Soviet empire. The August 1991 attempted coup against Gorbachev revealed the spectacle of Soviet disintegration to the world live on television and the defeat of those who wished to return to the past. Boris Yeltzin emerged as a hero that risked his life leading a democratic protest. The coup succeeded only in flaming the fires of democracy, which quickly spread beyond

Moscow and Leningrad. Gorbachev and the Communist Party were swept aside as the Soviet Union ceased to exist in December.

## *Conclusion*

The critics were wrong. Challenging Reagan's assumptions throughout his presidency, they consistently viewed his policies as simplistic and dangerous. In an *American History Magazine* article published in October 2003, Dinesh D'Souza recalled comments by foreign policy experts on Reagan.

Writing during the mid-1980's, Strobe Talbott, then a journalist at *Time* and later an official in the Clinton State Department, faulted officials in the Reagan administration for espousing "the early fifties goal of rolling back Soviet domination of Eastern Europe:, an objective he considered unrealistic and dangerous. "Reagan is counting on American technology and economic predominance to prevail in the end", Talbott scoffed, adding that if the Soviet economy was in a crisis of any kind "it is a permanent, institutionalized crisis with which the U.S.S.R. has learned to live."

Paul Boyer, Clifford Clark, Joseph Kett, Neal Salisbury, Harvard Sitkoff and Nancy Woloch, in their standard college American history text, *The Enduring Vision*, summarize Reagan's presidency with, "he had the good fortune to hold office as the Cold War thawed and the Soviet menace eased."[78]

William Perry in a similar standard college text, *Western Civilization: A Brief History (Fourth Edition)*, mentions Ronald Reagan twice in passing, while Gorbachev gets nearly three pages (and a photo). To be fair, however, Perry includes Gorbachev's failures as well as his achievements.

---

[78] Paul Boyer, Clifford Clark, Joseph Kett, Neal Salisbury, Harvard Sitkoff, Nancy Woloch, *The Enduring Vision: A History of the American People (Fifth Edition)* (New York: Houghton-Mifflin, 2004), 962.

Certainly, several disparate factors contributed to the end of the Cold War. Gorbachev's attempts to rescue the Soviet Union, internal pressures within the communist world, Margaret Thatcher's determined stand against communist, but most of all, Ronald Reagan's policies and his unwavering commitment stand out as essential. But for Reagan, Gorbachev might have succeeded.

## Chapter Five

# Desert Storm

*"First we're going to cut it off, and then we're going to kill it."*

General Colin Powell
Chairman, Joint Chiefs of Staff
(When asked about his strategy against the Iraqi Army)

Arab nationalism defined Iraq's existence during the Twentieth Century. Created as a British mandate out of the former Ottoman Empire at the end of World War I, Iraq experienced anti-British revolts in 1920 and 1922. Emir Faisal ibn Husayn, a Hashemite from Mecca was installed as the first king of Iraq through the influence of T. E. Lawrence. In 1927, huge oilfields were found near Kirkuk. When the British mandate ended in 1932, Iraq became nominally free. Faisal's son Ghazi became king in 1933. An avid sportsman, Ghazi managed to drive his car into a lamp post in 1939 and killed himself. His four year old son Faisal succeeded him as king.

In 1945, Iraq became a member of the new United Nations and a founding member of the Arab League. Mustafa Barzani, a Kurdish leader, led a failed rebellion against the national government in 1945. In the aftermath, Barzani fled to the Soviet Union to find sanctuary and support for future efforts on behalf of the Kurds.

During the 1948 war with Israel, Iraq supported the Arab cause. Iraq lost 50% of their oil revenues when the pipeline to Haifa (in Israel) was cut, seriously affecting the national economy. A mass exodus of Jews occurred after the hanging of a Jewish businessman in Iraq. Iraq joined the Baghdad Pact in 1956 that brought together Iraq, Turkey, Iran, Pakistan, the United States and the United Kingdom – an agreement designed to counter the growing Arab-nationalist influence of Egypt's Nasser. Jordan's King Hussein proposed a union of Hashemite monarchies to counter the Egyptian-Syrian union. Political activity associated with bringing this union together coincided with rising popular discontent with the Iraqi government. Influenced by Nasser, nationalistic Iraqi army officers overthrew and executed the king and his uncle, who had served as his regent. Iraq was declared a republic and withdrew from the Baghdad Pact. However, internal discontent within the new government continued.

Instability reigned with a series of coups bringing a Ba'ath party government into power in 1963, losing it to the army, then back to Ba'athist control again in 1968 under the leadership of General Ahmad Hassan al-Bakr. In 1961 when Kuwait was declared a free nation (it had been under British control), Iraq claimed Kuwait as Iraqi territory, but was deterred from making good on the claim by quick deployment of British troops.

With the return of Barzani to stir up Kurds in the north, the Ba'ath party General Secretary, Saddam Hussein engineered a political settlement with him in 1970. Under Ba'athist control, the economy began to stabilize, relations were restored with the United States, and Iraq participated in the 1973 war against Israel. Iraq also benefited from subsequent increase in oil prices and international prestige associated with the OPEC engineered oil crisis following the 1973 war. The country seemed energized and on track for success. Lingering difficulties with Kuwait and border problems with Iran interrupted progress to some extent.

In 1979, Saddam Hussein replaced al-Bakr as president and the head of the Ba'athist Revolutionary Command Council. After a promising decade under his predecessor, the 1980's marked a period of Iraqi decline under Saddam. A simmering border conflict with Iran blossomed into a war that lasted eight years (ending in 1988). With roots of the conflict between Iraq and Iran over control of the Khuzestan region of Iran going back to the Ottoman Empire, Saddam took the opportunity to exploit internal Iranian unrest associated with the Iranian Islamic revolution to invade Iran and attempt to seize Khuzestan.[79] The war quickly bogged down into front line assaults, reminiscent of the Western Front during World War I. The impact of the war on the Iraqi economy was devastating. The Soviet Union was Iraq's primary arms supplier during the war, providing modern fighter and bomber aircraft, helicopters, tanks, armored personnel carriers and the infamous Scud missiles. Also, Iraqi aircraft probably refueled at Soviet airfields. Because of the extensive use of Soviet equipment, the Iraqi Army adopted Soviet organization, doctrine and tactics. Other nations assisting Iraq during the war included France (in particular, with Mirage F-1 fighters), Switzerland, Czechoslovakia, Germany, Italy, Poland, Brazil, South Africa, Austria, Britain, and Sweden. The United States also supported Iraq against Iran because of the recent Iranian revolution, the Iranian hostage crisis and concern about growing Islamic fundamentalism. The US removed Iraq from the State Department list of terrorist supporting countries when the international terrorist Abu Nidal was exiled from Baghdad to Syria in 1983 and provided military aid at $200 million a year during the war (which was less than 1% of the total arms sold to Iraq during the war). During the war, Iraq was able to purchase anthrax from the US, sold for research, but usable to cultivate biological agents. Iraq also received $5 billion in economic aid from the United States from 1983 to 1990. During the latter part of the war, Iran began attacking merchant shipping in the Persian Gulf, particularly Kuwaiti tankers (because of Kuwait's support to Iraq). The United States initiated an operation to protect shipping in the Gulf by reflagging Kuwaiti tankers as US vessels and protecting them while in the Gulf region. During this operation, known as "Earnest Will", an Iraqi aircraft mistakenly launched two Exocet

---

[79] Khuzestan is a province in southwest Iran, along the Iranian border with Iraq. In ancient times, the area was known as Elam whose capital was Susa. The region is rich in resources, and was the subject of Iraqi-Iranian disputes of ownership ever since an ownership agreement was signed between Persia and the Ottoman Empire in 1639.

97

French built anti-ship missiles at the *USS Stark*, killing 27 sailors and wounding 21.

As the defacto leader of Iraq years before he became president, Saddam pursued the acquisition and use of weapons of mass destruction. Iraq's search for nuclear weapons was seriously interrupted by an Israeli air attack on the French built nuclear power plant at Osirak in 1981. Saddam's response to Israel's successful destruction of his nuclear facility was to execute the generals in charge of Iraqi air defenses. During the Iran-Iraq War, Saddam punished rebellious Kurds by attacking civilians, including the city of Halabja killing as many as 5,000 people with mustard gas and three types of nerve agents in 1988. Also during the war, Saddam's military used chemical weapons on Iranians, killing, according to Iranian sources, a total of 100,000 people.

The Iran-Iraq War ended in a stalemate in 1988. Saddam had borrowed heavily to finance military operations, assuming that his seizure of Khuzestan would provide an income that would more than make up for his expenditures. Consequently, Saddam found himself $14 billion in debt to Kuwait at the end of the war. Partially as a means to deflect attention from his debt problems and as a pretext to seize Kuwait, Iraq accused Kuwait of "slant drilling" (drilling from Kuwaiti surface to Iraqi underground oil reserves) and attempting to undercut oil prices to gain leverage in negotiating a border dispute with Iraq. Negotiations between Iraq and Kuwait were attempted in July 1990, but failed. When April Glaspie, the US Ambassador to Iraq met with Hussein on July 25, 1990, Hussein voiced complaints about Kuwait but indicated that he intended to continue talks to resolve their mutual issues. According to a transcript of the meeting published by the *New York Times,* on September 23, 1990 (the transcript was apparently leaked by the Iraqi government), Glaspie told Saddam that the US had no interest in a border dispute between Iraq and Kuwait. The *Times* reported her saying:

But we have no opinion on the Arab-Arab conflicts, like your border disagreement with Kuwait. I was in the American Embassy in Kuwait during the late '60's. The instruction we had during this period was that we should express no opinion on the issue and that the issue is not associated with America. James Baker (Secretary of State) has directed our official spokesmen to emphasize this instruction. We hope you can solve this problem using any suitable methods via Klibi (the Arab League General Secretary) or via President Mubarak (president of Egypt). All that we hope is that these issues are solved quickly.

Some inside and outside the US Government accused Glaspie of giving Saddam a green light for invasion, but in none of the three versions of the transcript that have surfaced since the meeting, does she agree or encourage an invasion, and in one transcript, she asks why Iraq is massing troops on the border. However it is possible that Saddam went ahead with the invasion because specific US statements of opposition were not voiced by the Ambassador.

Meanwhile, in the "Tank" (the Joint Chiefs of Staff[80] [JCS] briefing room) at the Pentagon, General Norman Schwarzkopf briefed the Joint Chiefs on the situation along the Kuwaiti border. Schwarzkopf was the Central Command (CENTCOM) Command in Chief[81] (CINC), and this was his part of the world

---

[80] The Joint Chiefs of Staff (JCS) consists of a Chairman, a Vice-Chairman, the Chief of Staff of the Army, Chief of Staff of the Air Force, Chief of Naval Operations and the Commandant of the Marine Corps. All of these officers are four star generals, and the four Service Chiefs are the senior military officers of their respective Services.

[81] The Department of Defense divides the world into regions, and establishes a senior Joint military command responsible for military operations within that region. Prior to George W. Bush's Administration, the military commander of each regional command was known as the "Commander in Chief" (CINC) for that command. Secretary Rumsfeld changed the regional commanders' designation to "Combatant Commander" because "there is only one commander-in-chief, and that is the President of the United States."

to watch. He told the assembled Service Chiefs that he didn't think an Iraqi buildup along the border was really a problem.[82]

Saddam invaded Kuwait on August 2, 1990. Three armored divisions composed of Soviet tanks and personnel carriers, using Soviet tactics drove into the heart of Kuwait down a highway built as a symbol of friendship between the two countries. Kuwaiti Hawk missiles systems were able to destroy 23 Soviet aircraft before their units were either overrun or destroyed. Despite Kuwaiti resistance, their small, lightly armed force was quickly overwhelmed. When UN sanctions were announced by the Security Council on August 6, Saddam annexed Kuwait as the "19th Province" of Iraq. The Kuwaiti ruling family and many citizens fled, primarily to Saudi Arabia. The United Nations Security Council passed a series of resolutions condemning Iraq for occupying Kuwait. Resolution 678 permitted the use of military force and set a deadline for Iraqi withdrawal from Kuwait by January 15, 1991. The US Congress eventually authorized the use of military force on January 12, 1991.

Saddam used this opportunity to call for Arabs to unite against the United States and Israel. It didn't work.

The immediate concern in the Bush Administration was that Iraq would continue to invade to the south, into Saudi Arabia and seize Saudi ports and oil fields. This concern was justified. Whereas Iraq owed Kuwait $14 billion, they owed Saudi Arabia $26 billion from their failed war with Iran. There were also some disagreements with Saudi Arabia over their mutual border. President Bush announced that the United States would conduct defensive operations against Iraq, and with Saudi approval, began deploying US troops.

---

[82] Richard T. Reynolds, *Heart of the Storm: The Genesis of the Air Campaign Against Iraq* (Maxwell Air Force Base: Air University Press, January 1995), 1.

## Operation "Desert Shield"

The United States Army was at the end of a long road of recovery following the Vietnam War. Reforms started by General Abrams during his short tenure as Chief of Staff (1972-1974) had taken effect. The Abrams Tank, the Bradley Fighting Vehicle, Black Hawk and Apache helicopters and the Patriot Missile System – all capabilities that Abrams championed – were to play significant roles during "Desert Storm". But most importantly, the Army culture had been reinvigorated with an influx of talented and very capable volunteer soldiers and officers and a return to basic military values. Trained relentlessly in realistic scenarios in brigade sized rotations at the National Training Center at Fort Irwin, California, the Army followed the Air Force's lead in demanding, challenging and unforgiving training. The payoff was America's uncharacteristic[83] winning of the first and only ground battle of "Desert Storm".

In early August at Schwarzkopf's CENTCOM headquarters at MacDill Air Force Base in Florida, at the XVIII Airborne Corps Headquarters at Fort Bragg in North Carolina, at the Ninth Air Force at Shaw Air Force Base in South Carolina, at the Pentagon and numerous other key joint headquarters locations, planners began reacting to JCS guidance to provide a blocking force to stop the Iraqis if and when they moved into Saudi Arabia. Everyone knew that ground forces wouldn't make it in time to stop a quick and determined attack – and air power was far away from the theater as well – but they were working on options.

---

[83] The United States Army had a habit of losing the first battles. The German defeat of the US Army at Kasserine Pass in February 1943 and North Korean defeat of "Task Force Smith" in South Korea in 1950 were taken to heart by the US Army. The Army leadership of the 1980's determined to win, not lose, the first battle of the next war and trained hard to attain that goal.

Generals Colin Powell (now Chairman of the Joint Chiefs of Staff) and Schwarzkopf met with the President and advisors on August 2 and laid out potential defensive options. The President, as a precautionary measure, ordered the *USS Independence* carrier battle group into the Gulf of Oman. By August 3, the President had concluded that some additional forces might be needed and upped the ante of naval power by ordering the *USS Eisenhower* carrier battle group to the Red Sea. On August 4, Schwarzkopf gave the President an update at Camp David. King Fahd of Saudi Arabia called the President shortly after Schwarzkopf's briefing and told him that he wanted a briefing on the situation. A team, led by Secretary of Defense Dick Cheney, went to the Saudi Arabia and briefed the King. After some discussion, King Fahd invited the US to deploy troops to Saudi Arabia to help defend the Kingdom on August 6. The US began moving troops and equipment on August 7, and on August 8 the President addressed the nation on the situation in Iraq. In his address, Bush gave the following reasons for committing US troops to the theater:

- Iraq invaded Kuwait without provocation with overwhelming forces just hours after Saddam assured the international community that he would not.
- Acquisition of territory by aggression is unacceptable.
- Protection of US lives abroad was paramount.

The 82nd Airborne Division[84] from Fort Bragg, NC began their airlift 36 hours after notification at 10:00 AM on August 8. At the same time, the XVIII Airborne Corps headquarters[85], also

---

[84] US Army divisions have between 15,000 and 20,000 troops assigned.

[85] Two Stinger air defense teams (two soldiers per team, plus a senior non-commissioned officer to supervise them) from my battalion, 2nd Battalion, 52nd Air Defense Artillery, deployed with the XVIII Airborne Corps headquarters. At that time, 2-52 ADA included about 650 soldiers. By the time the war ended in February, 1991, total assigned personnel peaked at about 800 (including two over-strength infantry platoons from the 9th Infantry Division, government civilian employees and contractors).

from Fort Bragg, began deployment. By October 1990, the 24th Infantry Division, 82nd Airborne Division, 101st Airborne (Air Assault) Division, 1st Calvary Division, 3rd Armored Calvary Regiment, Eastern Army Command (Arab Forces), Patriot and Hawk units from the 11th Air Defense Artillery Brigade, and the 1st and 7th Marine Expeditionary Brigades (meeting with their prepositioned equipment in Saudi Arabia) were in place. While the 82nd Airborne was moving, 24 F-15Cs from Langley Air Force Base, Virginia, began deployment to Saudi Arabia. Two days later, the British Royal Air Force (RAF) sent 24 Tornadoes and Jaguars to the Gulf. Within five days, the US Air Force moved a brigade of the 82nd, five fighter squadrons, and an Airborne Warning and Control System (AWACs) capability to the region.

As US forces began deployment, the Gulf Cooperation Council countries, Syria and Morocco reacted by beginning to contribute forces under the leadership of Egypt. The US Secretary of State worked to establish a coalition that eventually included 36 nations.

On August 22, President Bush authorized a call up of reservists to active duty for a period of 90 days. On November 12, the call up was broadened to 180 days.

By October (two months after Iraq's invasion of Kuwait), sufficient coalition forces were deployed in the theater to stop an Iraqi attack into Saudi Arabia. However, there wasn't enough combat power on the ground to force Saddam out of Kuwait. Throughout August and September, US and Coalition leadership knew that at some point, they would have to face the issue of getting Saddam out of Kuwait if diplomacy failed. Schwarzkopf's planners put together a plan that began with an air campaign followed by a ground attack. Ground planning began in earnest at the end of September, with the idea of driving the XVIII Airborne Corps into Kuwait from the south. Planners soon realized that they would need additional forces and raised the issue during a brief to the President on October 11. By

103

October 21, a plan to use two US Army corps was briefed to Schwarzkopf using a wide end around the Iraqi forces while the Arab forces and US Marines would attack to achieve limited objectives in the south of Kuwait. A fake amphibious landing of US Marines along the coast of Kuwait would keep Iraqi forces tied down and distracted while the real attack unfolded. Schwarzkopf obtained Powell's approval by October 23. The ground plan concept was in place, but planning continued until ground operations actually commenced in February. The President announced the deployment of the US VII Corps from Germany on November 8. The VII Corps commander, Lieutenant General Frederick Franks, Jr. anticipated a possible deployment in August and was well along in his contingency planning. Franks began movement to the Gulf on November 21 and completed on February 6, well after the start of the air campaign.

By the time the last units of VII Corps arrived, the total ground force available to the Coalition was formidable. The two corps were included 255,000 troops with about 2,000 tanks and about 1,600 fighting vehicles. The US Marines deployed a Marine Expeditionary Force composed of two divisions with 225 tanks, 882 fighting vehicles and 213 fixed wing combat aircraft. The Marine's total number of personnel in the theater was over 92,000. The US Navy deployed six aircraft carriers, 2 battleships, 11 guided missile cruisers and about 310 combat aircraft (fighters and bombers). The US Air Force deployed over 54,000 personnel, and 736 major combat aircraft (fighters and bombers). Coalition force contributions were also substantial. Great Britain deployed 42,000 ground and air force personnel with 180 tanks, 215 fighting vehicles and 84 fighter/bombers. France deployed 10,700 ground and air force personnel with 40 tanks, 120 armored vehicles and 58 fighter/bombers. Saudi Arabia provided 66,000 ground and air force personnel with 280 tanks, 950 fighting vehicles and 245 fighter/bombers. Egypt sent 30,200 ground personnel with 350 tanks and 750 fighting vehicles.  Syria provided 14,000 ground personnel with 240 tanks and 250 fighting vehicles.[86]

The Coalition faced the world's fourth largest army with eight years' recent experience in combat against Iran.  On paper, the Iraqi armed forces were formidable.  In truth, however, capabilities were very mixed.  The Republican Guard, Saddam's expanded handpicked palace guard, was the elite with the best Soviet equipment available – including latest versions of the T-72 tank.  Regular army heavy units had older equipment and were less motivated.  At the bottom were infantry divisions which were poorly equipped, trained, led and supported.  They were seen as cannon fodder by both sides.  The Iraqi Air Force was equipped with modern French and Soviet equipment, but spent most of the war trying to keep from being destroyed.[87] Iraqi ground forces were composed of 1,100,000 personnel in 66 divisions (including 8 Republican Guard division) with approximately 6,000 tanks, 11,200 armored fighting vehicles and 110 surface to surface missile launchers (including Scuds). Within the Kuwaiti Theater of Operations (KTO – the area immediately in and around Kuwait), Iraqi forces included 4280 tanks, 2880 armored fighting vehicles and 3100 artillery pieces.[88] The Iraqi Air Force had 18,000 personnel with about 750 fighter/bombers.[89]

## Operation "Desert Storm"

Coalition planners developed a four phased operation.  The first three phases were part of a deliberate air campaign against the Iraqi strategic defense structure.  Phase I was a strategic air campaign comprised of striking Iraqi command and control

---

[86] Coalition force information taken from Anthony Cordesman, *Lessons of Modern War – Volume IV – The Gulf War*, (Center for Strategic and International Studies, October 15, 1994), 126.
[87] Scales, 113.
[88] "Conduct of the Persian Gulf War: Final Report to Congress", US Department of Defense, April 1992, 308.
[89] Cordesman, 126.

facilities, weapons of mass destruction facilities, and Republican Guard units. Phase II involved the suppression of enemy air defenses (SEAD). Phase III included striking military ground targets within the area of operation. The fourth and final phase was the ground attack to remove Iraq from Kuwait.[90] (See Figure 3)

> The first irretrievable hostile fire in Operation "Desert Storm" began at approximately 0130 (H-90 minutes), 17 January, when US warships launched Tomahawk land attack missiles (TLAMs) toward Baghdad. At 0238, while the TLAMs were still in flight, helicopters attacked early warning radar sites in southern Iraq. Stealth fighters already had passed over these sites enroute to attack targets in western Iraq and Baghdad. . . Powerful air strikes then continued throughout the country. Within hours, key parts of the Iraqi leadership, C2 (command and control) networks, strategic air defense systems, and the NBC (nuclear, biological and chemical) warfare capabilities were neutralized.[91]

Coalition air power, led by US Air Force, US Navy, US Army, US Marine Corps and British Royal Air Force (RAF) aircraft flew more than 1,000 sorties[92] per day. Some sorties included precision munitions, but most of the bombs used throughout the war were "dumb" bombs – free fall bombs whose accuracy depended on air crew skill, not on precision guidance. By the start of the ground campaign, the Department of Defense reported that Coalition air forces claimed incapacitation of 1,772 tanks, 948 armored personnel carriers and 1,474 artillery pieces.[93] Contemporary analysis and subsequent review of air destruction of combat equipment before the ground war dispute

---

[90] "Conduct of the Persian Gulf War: Final Report to Congress", 140.
[91] Ibid., 141.
[92] A "sortie" is "one mission or attack by a single plane", *Merriam Webster's Collegiate Dictionary (Tenth Edition),* (Springfield, Massachusetts: Merriam-Webster, Inc, 1993).
[93] "Conduct of the Persian Gulf War: Final Report to Congress", 192.

these numbers. For example, of the 800 Republican Guard tanks in the theater, by the end of the air campaign, the Defense Intelligence Agency (DIA) estimated that only about 25 had been destroyed by air attacks.[94] Saddam launched some of his air force early in the war, resulting in 38 MIGs[95] being shot down. Soon, Iraqi Air Force pilots began escaping to Iran. Saddam also began launching Scud missiles into Saudi Arabia and Israel.

During the course of the war, Iraq would launch 88 Scud missiles with 46 heading toward various targets in the Coalition operating area and the other 42 fired at Israel. Although generally intercepted by Patriots or ineffective upon impact, one Scud attack killed 28 American soldiers in Dhahran on February 25, 1991. The missiles used by Iraq were variations of standard Soviet Scud missiles. The Iraqis attempted to reduce payload and gain additional range with modifications, but design flaws caused the missiles to breakup upon entry into the atmosphere, making engagement by Patriot missiles difficult.

While air operations were ongoing, Schwarzkopf began a complex shift of ground forces into the western desert to line up two powerful corps composed of the equivalent of 17 combat divisions in preparation for the ground phase. The two corps commanders, Lieutenant General Gary Luck (XVIII Airborne Corps) and Franks would have two weeks to move more than 64,000 wheeled and tracked vehicles and 225,000 soldiers as much as 300 miles to the west. At the same time, they had to coordinate all of the logistical support (ammunition, food, fuel, water, and repair parts) for the move and subsequent combat operations.

---

[94] Rick Atkinson, *Crusade: The Untold Story of the Persian Gulf War*, (New York: Houghton-Mifflin, 1993), 161.
[95] A MIG is an aircraft built by the Mikoyan Gurevich (shortened to "MIG") Soviet design bureau. Iraq possessed capable, late model MIG aircraft including the MIG-25 (an interceptor fielded in 1969) and MIG-29 (a fighter aircraft comparable to the US F/A-18 Hornet that entered Soviet service in 1983).

Before the start of ground operations, Iraqi forces attempted an attack in Al-Khafji, a town in northeast Saudi Arabia. Arab forces supported by US Marines pushed the invading Iraqis back into Kuwait. This attack, and a similar Iraqi operation near Al-Wafrah, was costly to Iraqis, and reinforced confidence among the US Marine and coalition forces. The Iraqi Army (built up by international press) wasn't as formidable as advertised.

The ground campaign began on February 24 after 38 days of air attacks. Objectives for the ground campaign were: to drive the Iraqi's out of Kuwait, destroy the Republican Guard forces within the theater, and restore the Kuwaiti government.[96] Iraq prepared two defensive belts and defensive structures along the Gulf consistent with how they operated during the Iran-Iraq War. At the beginning of the ground campaign, Saddam's command and control structure had been seriously degraded by the air campaign, affecting his ability to direct ground forces. In addition, a Marine force sat off the coast of Kuwait threatening an invasion and tying down three Iraqi divisions that could have been used against Marine and Arab forces attacking toward Kuwait City from the south.

At 0400 on February 24, simultaneous ground operations began in three places. In the far west, the 6th French Light Division and 101st Airborne Division began an air-ground sweep into the desert far west of Kuwait 280 kilometers up to the Euphrates River to cut Iraqi routes of retreat. In the center, the 1st Calvary Division feinted an attack up the Wadi Al-Batin. In the east 1st Marine Expeditionary Force (MEF) and Joint Force Command East (JFC-E – composed of forces from Saudi Arabia, United Arab Emirates, Oman, Qatar, Bahrain and Kuwait) attacked north into Kuwait. At 1500, the 1st Infantry Division conducted a breach operation to the west of the 1st Calvary Division. Joint Force Command North (JFC-N – composed of

---

[96] "Conduct of the Persian Gulf War: Final Report to Congress", 274.

Egyptian, Syrian, Saudi and Kuwaiti forces) began an attack at 1600 on February 24 into Kuwait.

The VII Corps was responsible to deal with Iraqi Republican Guard units. A series of battles developed beginning on February 26 between VII Corps units and the Republican Guard. These included the Battle of Wadi Al-Batin (which included $2^{nd}$ Armored Calvary Regiment's famous "Battle of 73 Easting"), in which the VII Corps destroyed the Republican Guard's Tawakalna Division, and the Battle of Medina Ridge where the Republican Guard Medina Division attempted to ambush the US $1^{st}$ Armored Division. The Iraqi's lost over 300 tanks. Beginning on 24 February, I MEF attacked toward Kuwait City, then stood aside for Kuwaiti and other Arab forces to enter the city at the insistence of Schwarzkopf. By the morning of February 27, Arab troops were poised to liberate Kuwait City.

As Iraqi troops attempted to flee Kuwait City to the north, they were attacked from the air, leaving hundreds of vehicles destroyed, although most of the occupants had fled into the desert to avoid being killed. General Powell, when viewing aerial photographs of bombed and burnt out vehicles along the road leading out of Kuwait City back in the Pentagon, considered the destruction over the top and urged the President to declare a cease fire. He also believed, along with Secretary of Defense Cheney, that the military objectives had been achieved. At the President's request, Powell called Schwarzkopf for his view on a cease fire. Lieutenant General John Yeosock, the US Third Army commander in charge of US Army ground forces, had requested one additional day to complete the destruction of Republican Guard forces, but his request was not strongly pursued by Schwarzkopf when was talking with Powell. Consequently, the decision was made at the White House to cease operations, although Republican Guard units were still escaping the incomplete coalition encirclement. A cease fire took effect at 0800, February 28. The decision to end the war without the destruction or surrender of all Republican Guard units (at least three divisions escaped), along with

109

Schwarzkopf's decision to allow the Iraqi's to use helicopters in the aftermath of the war (supposedly to move key personnel) were both widely criticized after the war.

The coalition captured nearly 70,000 Iraqi prisoners, destroyed 3,700 of 4,280 tanks, 2,400 of 2,880 armored personnel carriers and 2,600 of 3,100 artillery pieces.[97] The Iraqi air force was destroyed or grounded, but the tactical ballistic missile (such as "Scud" missiles) mobile launch capability was virtually intact, with more than 100 Scud missiles surviving. About one third of the Iraqi Army and one half of the Republican Guard units escaped destruction.[98]

## *Post War Iraq*

Unlike the end of World War II in Europe, the coalition did not demand unconditional surrender. The immediate goals of ejecting Iraq from Kuwait and restoration of the Kuwaiti government were achieved. Destruction of the Republican Guard was not. The removal of Saddam was not an official goal of the US or other coalition nations. He was left in power and put on a leash that he managed to slip out of in the coming decade.

In the middle of February, 1991, President Bush urged Iraqis to overthrow Saddam. The suppressed Shi'ite majority in the south took Bush's advice and tried to do just that – expecting US help. Because the Iraqi military was allowed to use their helicopters (agreed to by Schwarzkopf at the cease fire talks), the Iraqi Army was able to put down the Shi'ite revolt in the south, with bloody consequences. Washington did not react to assist the revolt because Iran expressed support for the Shi'ites, even though there was little or no linkage between Iraqi Shi'ites and the Iranian regime at the time. Bitterness in the south at the US

---

[97] Central Command Report as described by Global Security at http://www.globalsecurity.org/military/world/iraq/ground-equipment-intro.htm. Accessed August 15, 2005.
[98] Atkinson, 495.

failure to come to their aid would be a factor in the next Iraqi war. A similar situation was close to developing in the North. Ethnic Kurds, traditional enemies of Saddam, rebelled. Iraqi Army units moved north to suppress the rebellion. Eventually President Bush bowed to European pressure and agreed to send US troops to help create a protected enclave in the north. American, British and French warplanes flew patrol over the north to prevent Iraqi attacks above the 36th parallel.[99]

Saddam was left with ballistic missiles and weapons of mass destruction (WMD) capabilities. Iraq retained more than 20 facilities to work on their version of the Manhattan project after the war. During the ensuing years, the United Nations placed weapons inspectors in Iraq to inventory, then destroy Saddam's weapons systems as outlined in the April 1991 cease fire agreement.

Within two years of the war, George Bush was voted out of office. Margaret Thatcher was no longer Britain's Prime Minister. But Saddam Hussein was still in Baghdad, and finding ways to get around UN sanctions to line his own pockets.

## Gulf War Illness

Following "Desert Storm", approximately 100,000 American veterans began experiencing various symptoms that have collectively been called "Gulf War Illness" or "Gulf War Syndrome". Symptoms included debilitating fatigue, intermittent fever, night sweats, serious joint pain, muscle pain, and short term memory loss.[100] The US Department of Defense established a task force in 1995 to investigate potential causes of these collective illnesses in order to aid in treatment. The task force concluded that troops deployed to the Gulf were exposed to various types of chemicals, including: pesticides, chemicals

---

[99] Atkinson, 489.
[100] "Gulf War Illness Research" http://www.immed.org/illness/gulfwar _illness_research.html. Accessed August 16, 2005.

associated with Iraqi Scud missiles, mustard and nerve agents released from the destruction of munitions at an Iraqi ammunition storage facility, the oil well fires set by the Iraqis during the war, and radiation released in low levels from depleted uranium rounds. In addition, soldiers were required to take anti-nerve agent pills (many, if not most, of which were expired), anthrax shots and other immunizations that may contribute to these symptoms. Gulf War Illness is not a single disease, but has a combination of causes with long term affects.

The treatment and rehabilitation of veterans with Gulf War Illness remains a focus within the Veteran's Administration and a veteran's issue for a number of organizations. One of the unintended consequences of warfare is the long term health of veterans – an issue the nation has had to deal with at the end of each war.

## *Conclusion*

Rick Atkinson in his classic history of "Desert Storm", *Crusade: The Untold Story of the Persian Gulf War*, summarized general results of the war. He concluded that although Norman Schwarzkopf made mistakes, drew incorrect conclusions and had marginal impact on the air campaign, he was able to pull together a diverse coalition forces to win the war and encourage initiative in subordinate commanders. Atkinson stated that the air campaign had little strategic effect on the war because it was too short (unlike endless months of bombing Germany during World War II), but it helped to shock and demoralize Iraqi troops on the ground prior to the start of the ground campaign. He believes that the bond between America's military and the civil population had been reaffirmed (after long darkness following Vietnam). Atkinson states that the Bush Administration was able to pull together a remarkable and diverse coalition, composed of former Cold War enemies. Finally, he concluded that Saddam Hussein was defanged – his Army was reduced, subsequent UN inspections began to dismantle his WMD and ballistic missile inventory and he was under economic sanctions.[101] Atkinson's book, written in 1993, preceded a decade of UN based corruption that Saddam was able to use to enrich himself and a select few within the UN, his entourage and his favorite international corporations. Furthermore, Saddam demonstrated great resilience and resourcefulness in facing down the West over the next decade.

---

[101] Atkinson, 494-495.

## Chapter Six

# America's Wars of the 1990's

*"What's the point of having this superb military that you're always talking about if we can't use it?"*

Madeline Albright
Then US Ambassador to the United Nations

*"Spend my life if you have to, but don't waste it"*

A Warrior's Creed

*"The only mission of an infantry soldier is to kill the enemy. 'Humanitarian missions' are someone else's job."*

Major Mark Smith
Green Beret, Former POW

Even before the beginning of "Desert Storm", many in and around Washington were talking about a "peace dividend" – a windfall of funds made available by reducing defense expenditures that were believed no longer necessary due to the end of the Cold War. From 1990 to 2000, the Presidents Bush and Clinton, along with Congress, cut the US Army from 780,800 active duty troops to 480,000 – nearly a 40% reduction. At the same time, the number of troop deployments to conflicts and peace keeping duties went up by 300%.[102] Comparable reductions in other military services (except the already small Marine Corps) also took place during this decade. Against a back drop of a smaller and often overworked military, the wars of the 1990's unfolded.

---

[102] Joseph Cyrulik and Wolf Kutter, "Army Endstrength and the National Security Strategy", *National Security Watch*, Institute of Land Warfare, 8 July 1999, 1.

# Black Hawk Down – the Battle of Mogadishu

Mark Bowden's book, *Black Hawk Down* and the movie of the same title immortalized combat in the streets of Mogadishu in October 1993. The events surrounding the battle fought on October 3 are not as well known, nor are the long term impacts of that day on the "War on Terror" to follow eight years later.

In January 1991, Somalian dictator Siad Barre was removed from office and anarchy and civil war followed, characterized by factional infighting, famine and starvation. In March 1992, the various warring factions in Somalia agreed to a ceasefire that included UN monitoring and humanitarian aid. However, once the UN mission was in place, the security situation in Somalia began to deteriorate. Armed gunmen looted humanitarian support cargo as soon as the aircraft landed. Food convoys were attacked and aid workers assaulted. The UN requested security assistance from member nations, and President George H. W. Bush responded by offering 25,000 troops. On December 9, US Marines landed on the beach at Mogadishu into the bright lights of network news television cameras (causing many to wonder what would have happened to all of those reporters if the Marines were fired upon). Bush told the nation that the purpose of the deployment was to provide a secure environment and that the operation would be turned over to the UN as soon as the situation was stabilized. UN Secretary General Boutros Boutros-Ghali demanded that Bush disarm the warlords, but Bush refused, limiting the US military mission to securing the humanitarian assistance operations. Bush was aware that Boutros-Ghali had a history with one of the most powerful warlords, General Mohammed Farah Aidid, and refused to do Boutros-Ghali's bidding in disarming him. By March 1993, the food delivery operations appeared to be stabilized.

On May 4, 1993 the UN took over operations from the United States. At the same time, newly installed President Bill Clinton scaled back the number of US combat troops in the country. Meanwhile, the UN expanded the mandate from humanitarian aid to rebuilding the economy and political institutions. Madeline Albright, the American ambassador to the United Nations, said that the goal was the "restoration of an entire country". Aidid, the aforementioned warlord who was an enemy of the UN Secretary General, had plans of his own, and took exception to the UN intent.

On June 5, armed Somalis attacked and massacred Pakistani UN peacekeepers. Aidid was blamed for the attack. Admiral Jonathan Howe, the Special Representative of the UN Secretary General, placed a $25,000 reward on Aidid's head and requested a US counter-terrorist unit be sent to Somalia to find Aidid. In mid-June 1993, US and UN troops began looking for Aidid – putting the "peacekeepers" at war with the warlord. Essentially Admiral Howe had turned the peacekeepers into a posse. On July 12, US Cobra attack helicopters were used by UN forces to attack a house in Mogadishu where clan leaders were meeting. Between 20 and 50 Aidid lieutenants were killed and four Western journalists who arrived to cover the story were beaten to death. This attack, which was supposed to remove Aidid as a powerbroker only emboldened him. On August 8, four US military policemen were killed by a remotely detonated explosive device (a foretaste of what would come in Iraq). Two weeks later, six more soldiers were wounded.

Under pressure from Boutros-Ghali to send troops to find Aidid and from Howe, who specifically requested the US to send a Delta Force[103] element, Secretary of Defense Les Aspin sent a total of 440 Delta Force personnel, US Army Rangers and elements of 160th Special Operations Aviation Regiment (collectively known as "Task Force Ranger") to Mogadishu on August 26 with the mission of capturing Aidid. Aspin's decision was taken against the advice of his military leaders. The deputy UN commander, US Army Major General Thomas Montgomery,

---

[103] "Delta Force", officially known as the 1st Special Forces Operational Detachment – Delta (SFOD-D) was established in 1977 to deal with terrorist organizations and/or incidents. The unit is highly selective, recruiting and testing only highly qualified Special Forces operators.

later said during a Senate investigation that he had specifically requested British Special Forces instead of Americans. "Task Force Ranger" was commanded by Major General William Garrison. At the same time that "Task Force Ranger" was looking for Aidid, the Clinton Administration opened secret negotiations with him, using former president Jimmy Carter as the intermediary. Carter made contact with Aidid in mid-September and reported to Clinton that Aidid was ready to negotiate to end the fighting. Military commanders in Somalia were not told of these negotiations.

Montgomery concluded that additional capabilities were required to accomplish his mission and requested armored vehicles and AC-130[104] aircraft to support "Task Force Ranger". Secretary Aspin denied the request even though it was supported by Chairman of Joint Chiefs Powell. Aspin didn't want to appear to be building up US forces while they were actually being reduced (failing to learn a lesson from Vietnam). Aspin's decision ensured that "Task Force Ranger" would not have an armored rescue capability or heavy firepower immediately available – and that they would have to rely on UN forces for assistance if they got into trouble.

On October 3, "Task Force Ranger" received intelligence that several of Aidid's lieutenants would be meeting in the Olympic Hotel in Mogadishu. They assaulted the hotel and captured the lieutenants. In the process, however, one helicopter was shot down by Aidid faction members with a rocket propelled grenade (RPG). The helicopter crashed. Rangers were sent by the on-scene commander to secure the crash sight several blocks away. Then the helicopter sent to replace the one that crashed was also shot down. The fire-fight between the Rangers and Aidid's militia dragged on because Garrison had no armored

---

[104] The AC-130 is a four-engine cargo aircraft reconfigured as a powerful gunship. Armament includes 105 millimeter howitzer, 40 and 25 millimeter cannons and a sophisticated fire control system. The AC-130 can deliver tremendous, accurate firepower in a concentrated area very quickly.

vehicles available to rescue the troops pinned down in the city. A total of 18 Rangers and Delta Force personnel were killed, and 73 wounded. Two Delta Force snipers, Master Sergeant Gary Gordon and Sergeant First Class Randy Shughart received posthumous Medals of Honor for their attempt to rescue the pilot of the second aircraft shot down. Somali's dragged American bodies through the streets in front of TV cameras. The pilot that Gordon and Shughart attempted to rescue, Michael Durant, was taken prisoner and held by Aidid until October 14. Ultimately, Garrison requested assistance from the 10th Mountain Division (the US Army peacekeeping unit in Mogadishu under the UN) and Pakistani and Malaysian armored vehicles to extract "Task Force Ranger" personnel.

President Clinton announced on October 7 that US troops would be fully withdrawn by March 1994. His hunt for Aidid was called off and US representatives were sent to negotiate with him. Two months after the battle, US soldiers escorted Aidid to the Mogadishu airport to fly him to Addis Ababa in a US aircraft. In answering questions about why Aidid was given VIP treatment only weeks after the battle, President Clinton responded that American soldiers had died fighting for "peace" and had "achieved their objective".

Aidid died in August 1995 from gunshot wounds received during an outbreak of fighting. Aspin, who had been a vociferous critic of the US military as a Congressman (and whose appointment as Secretary of Defense was as about as welcome in the Pentagon as a thumb in the eye), resigned as Secretary of Defense in December 1993 (actually leaving office in February 1994). He died in 1995 after suffering a stroke.

Osama bin Laden's organization, based in Sudan, was involved in training militia members fighting UN and US troops in Somalia during 1992 and 1993. The Clinton Administration's indictment against bin Laden, issued in 1998 includes the following charge:

On October 3 and 4, 1993, in Mogadishu, Somalia, persons who had been trained by al Qaeda (and by trainers trained by al Qaeda) participated in an attack on United States military personnel serving in Somalia as part of Operation Restore Hope, which attack resulted in the killing of 18 United States Army personnel .. [105]

Lasting effects resulted from the Battle of Mogadishu. Aidid expected immediate retribution for American losses. So did the Rangers on the ground. However, the president had enough and withdrew American forces. For al Qaeda and other interested parties, the lesson learned was that the United States didn't have the will to complete the mission. They saw that the US chose to withdraw instead of pursuing their enemies and assumed they could count on the US to continue this kind of behavior in the future.

The Clinton Administration became "gun-shy" of American losses, and US armed forces were required to adopt a policy of "force protection", with commanders being held accountable for making decisions that would result in personnel losses. Future operations during the Clinton Administration were characterized by high altitude bombing or cruise missile strikes instead of direct ground force intervention.

The UN leadership learned that the US was willing to spend the lives of US soldiers pursuing UN interests, not those of the United States. [106]

On a personal note, I was acquainted with Randy Shughart (Delta Force sniper killed attempting to rescue Michael Durant) while assigned to Fort Bragg as a battalion commander. He was a friend of some of my junior officers and highly regarded by all who knew him. I first learned of the battle and his death while in

---

[105] "US Charges Relating to Osama Bin Laden's Connection to the 1993 Mogadishu Attack", www.pbs.org/wgbh/pages/frontline/shows/ambush/readings/indictment.html. Accessed August 16, 2005.

[106] Jed Babbin, "Clinton's Classroom" *National Review*, June 29, 2004.

my office at the Pentagon. I was aware of Montgomery's request for armor support and knew that Secretary Aspin had denied it. Sometime after the battle, a friend that worked in another office on the Army staff took me aside and showed me a POW medal along with an award citation that she was holding in her desk. The citation had Michael Durant's name on it. She told me that Secretary Aspin had refused to sign the award because Durant was taken prisoner in a peacekeeping operation, instead of during "wartime". As far as the Secretary of Defense was concerned, Shughart had selflessly given his life trying to save a soldier from armed gunmen during a "peacekeeping operation". My friend later told me that General Gordon Sullivan, US Army Chief of Staff and Acting Secretary of the Army signed the award anyway.

## Bosnia-Herzegovina

War descended on Bosnia and Herzegovina (commonly shortened to Bosnia) in 1992. Bosnia is part of the former Yugoslavia, a state created by melding portions of the Ottoman and Austrian empires in the wake of World War I. The Bosnian war of 1992-1995 was part of the larger disintegration of Yugoslavia following the death of strongman Marshal Josip Tito in 1980.

The other five former republics of Yugoslavia were composed primarily of majority ethnic groups, and as the nation began to fall apart, ethnic majorities were able to create relatively homogeneous states – beginning with Slovenia in 1991, followed quickly by Croatia. Bosnia, however, is composed of three primary ethnic groups with no clear majority among them. These groups include: Bosnian Muslims (also known as "Bosniaks"), Bosnian Serbs (Eastern Orthodox) and Croats (Roman Catholic). The history of infighting among these ethnic groups is deeply rooted – going back to rivalries associated with the Turkish domination of the Balkans followed by Austrian control (after 1878) and formal Austrian annexation (1908), then the events leading up to World War I including the assassination of Austrian Archduke Franz Ferdinand by Serbian nationalists in Sarajevo (capital of Bosnia) on June 27, 1914. Following World War I, Bosnia became part of the "Kingdom of Serbs, Croats and Slovenes", mercifully renamed "Yugoslavia" in 1929. During World War II, the Germans that occupied Yugoslavia used the puppet state of Croatia to control the region. World War II also brought fighting among the ethnic groups as they lined up to fight for or against the Axis powers.

After Slovenian and Croatian declarations of independence and resulting war with the Yugoslav Army in 1991, Bosnia held a referendum on independence (boycotted by Bosnian Serbs who wished to stay part of Serbian controlled Yugoslavia) in February and March 1992. A Bosnian republic was declared on April 5, 1992. The Bosnian Serbs declared an independent republic on April 7. War for control of the country consequently erupted among the three "warring factions". While the Yugoslav Army attempted to suppress independence, each of the three factions formed their own military organizations. The resulting war was the most widespread and destructive in Europe since World War II. Various peace initiatives were proposed, including a widely publicized plan by Cyrus Vance and David Owen[107] (*Vance-Owen*) in 1992 which failed. The UN Security Council expanded an existing peace force in Croatia in June 1992 to cover Bosnia and aid in delivery of humanitarian aid and protect civilian refugees.

Initially, the Bosniaks and Croats worked together against the Serbs, but after the failure of the *Vance-Owen* plan, they began fighting with each other as well. However, Bosniaks and Croats signed an agreement in 1994 in Washington establishing the Federation of Bosnia and Herzegovina and began, at least nominally, to coordinate their military activities.

---

[107] Cyrus Vance was Secretary of State under President Carter. Lord David Anthony Llewellen Owen was British Foreign Secretary under Labor Party Prime Minister James Callaghan.

The UN passed sanctions to stop importation of arms, which included a Western European Union (WEU) and NATO naval blockade codenamed "Sharp Guard" in 1993. In 1993, NATO also began operation "Deny Flight" to enforce a no-fly zone over Bosnia and to provide close air support to UN forces. The UN also requested that NATO develop a series of emergency withdrawal plans for UN forces in the event that it was necessary to extract UN or non-governmental organization personnel from Bosnia under extreme situations. Accordingly, a NATO team was assembled in August and September 1994 at Allied Forces Southern Europe (AFSOUTH) headquarters in Naples, Italy, to plan and coordinate emergency rescue operations.[108] NATO (including the US) was thus was drawn further and deeper into the conflict. Both Secretary of State Warren Christopher and President Bill Clinton argued that unless the United States engaged in the Bosnian conflict, the potential existed for it to spread to other parts of Europe (the "domino theory" revised from the justification for going into Vietnam). Former British Prime Minister Margaret Thatcher argued that would-be dictators would be deterred by a NATO show of force in Bosnia.

On August 27, 1994, Lieutenant General Wesley Clark, then in charge of strategic planning for the US Joint Chiefs of Staff, visited Bosnia. Although warned by a senior official at NATO's headquarters for the southern region in Naples, Italy not to visit the Bosnian Serb commander, General Ratko Mladic, Clark did so anyway.[109] During this visit, two incidents occurred – one was an embarrassment to the Administration, the other revealed American foreign policy intentions that undercut NATO policy on Bosnia.

---

[108] The NATO planning team was led by myself and included experienced US Army, US Air Force, British Army, and Dutch Army planners, supplemented at various times by French and Canadian officers.
[109] Elaine Grossman, "Fellow Military Leaders May Provide to be Clark's Toughest Hurdle", *Inside the Pentagon*, September 17, 2003.

First, Clark allowed himself to be persuaded to exchange hats with Mladic (who was to be indicted as a war criminal eleven months later) and to be photographed in the process. Unfortunately for Clark, that photograph was widely circulated in European papers. Clark also accepted Mladic's gift of his personal pistol. After the meeting, when Clark was exiting Croatia through the airport in Zagreb, Croatian authorities discovered the hat and pistol. After three hours, Clark and his entourage were released. Reports differ as to whether Clark was allowed to keep the articles.[110] The second aspect of Clark's visit underscored the Clinton Administration's intent regarding Bosnia. During a meeting with the Bosniak president, Alijo Izetbegovic, Clark discussed the possibility that the United States "would consider breaking its arms embargo by providing weapons to the Muslims."[111] Clark asked Izetbegovic if Bosnian Muslim forces could use American weapons. This offer was made at a time when the presence of Iranian terrorist training camps was widely reported in the Muslim held areas of Bosnia.

After Clark's visit, the embargo remained in place, but the US government authorized the Croatian government to sign a contract with a US company composed of retired military personnel to provide military training support to the Croatian military. With their newly found skills honed by American military experts, the Croats launched an extremely effective operation against the Serbs in the summer of 1995. But the summer of 1995 also saw the Bosnian Serb army on the move.

Early in the conflict, several Muslim enclaves in eastern Bosnia were surrounded by Bosnian Serb forces. UN peacekeepers were put in place to protect these enclaves. At the town of Srebrenica, a Dutch peacekeeping battalion composed of 350 soldiers was responsible to protect the Muslim population. Ultimately, not only did the Bosnian Serbs hold the Muslims

---

[110] Published reports said Clark had to leave the hat and pistol behind. An individual involved in the incident at the airport told me that Clark took the hat and pistol.

[111] Grossman.

hostage, but the Dutch peacekeepers as well. By May 1995, General Janvier, the UN commander requested that the Dutch battalion be reinforced or withdrawn, but the UN headquarters ignored his request. In May and June, the Bosnian Serbs, sensing they had the upper hand, cut off humanitarian convoys, sealing off the city. On July 9, the Bosnian Serbs took 30 Dutch peacekeepers hostage as future bargaining chips. By July 10, as Bosnian Serbs closed on the city, the Dutch battalion commander requested NATO air support to help stop the Bosnian Serb advance but his request was denied by Janvier. After another request, late on July 10, Janvier agreed to provide air strikes against Bosnian Serb forces at 0600, July 11. However, at 0900 the next morning (three hours after the air strike was supposed to happen), Janvier notified the Dutch commander that his request for air support was submitted on an incorrect form and that it must be resubmitted. Meanwhile, NATO aircraft were on station waiting for permission to strike, but they were forced to circle the city as Serbs advanced. Clearance finally came from the UN at 1200, but by that time, NATO aircraft had returned to base in Italy because they were low on fuel. Dutch F-16's finally dropped bombs on the Bosnian Serbs, but the Serbs threatened to kill Dutch hostages unless the bombing stopped. The Dutch battalion commander abandoned further resistance and Mladic (the general who exchanged hats with Clark) entered the city in triumph. The Dutch battalion commander surrendered Muslims that had taken refuge in the Dutch battalion enclave and the Serbs promptly separated women and children from the men. They sent women and children on buses to a Muslim held area while the men were executed. Approximately 7,000 men were killed between July 12 and July 16, 1995. The Bosnian Serbs allowed the Dutch battalion to leave Srebrenica on July 16.

The UN's actions at Srebrenica were a microcosm of their approach to peacekeeping in Bosnia. Small battalions scattered across the country were restricted in their ability to function militarily, and also suffered from a culture of passivity in the face of aggression from leaders of the three warring factions. In addition, they had to deal with independent warlords who masqueraded as warring faction officers, but seized humanitarian aid for sale on the black market in exchange for passage on roads or bridges that they controlled. Some peacekeeping units were ill equipped, often from Third World countries, and some were continually on the verge of becoming hostages.

On August 28, 1995, explosion(s) in an open air market in Sarajevo killed 37 and wounded at least 80 people. Bosniaks and the UN immediately blamed the Bosnian Serbs for dropping mortar rounds on the market. Subsequent analysis, by British, French and Russian officers indicated that a single mortar round was probably dropped by the Muslims[112] on their own marketplace.[113] The presumption is that this would encourage NATO action against the Serbs – something already predicted by US Ambassador Richard Holbrook the day before the attack.

NATO did begin attacks on the Bosnian Serbs. Operation "Deliberate Force," put together by NATO air planners over a period of several months, was executed on August 29, 1995. The bombing campaign was designed to reduce the military capabilities of the Bosnian Serb forces. NATO pilots struck selected targets until September 14, when the warring factions agreed to cease fire conditions established by the UN.

Peace negotiations took place at Wright-Patterson Air Force Base at Dayton, Ohio. The peace accords were initialed by representatives of the three warring factions (Bosnian Croats, Bosnian Serbs and Bosnian Muslims), Croatia and Serbia (Former Yugoslavia) on November 21, 1995. The agreement was signed in Paris on December 14, 1995.

---

[112] David Binder, "Beyond the Pale: Perspectives from Two Serbias", *Mediterranean Quarterly*, Spring 1996. In addition to this reference, when I went to the marketplace following the implementation of the *Dayton Peace Accords*, I was told that French analysts had reached the same conclusion – that no Serb artillery or mortar pieces were positioned in such a way to reach the precise location of the explosion.
[113] David Hackworth, "Bombs over Bosnia Failed Bigtime" *Defending America,* September 5, 1995.

A NATO peace implementation force (IFOR) composed of 60,000 troops took over from the UN in December 1995 with a one-year mandate. A follow-on stabilization force (SFOR), remains in Bosnia (as of 2005) with approximately 20,000 troops.

American involvement in the Bosnian war reveals continuity and change in the Clinton foreign policy. During Somalia, the Administration allowed itself to be used by the UN Secretary General to pursue a personal agenda. In the case of Bosnia, the Administration used the UN to achieve their own aim – to ensure the success of the Bosnian Muslims. Throughout the course of the Bosnian conflict, the United States consistently demonstrated an anti-Serb bias through efforts to support Croatia (with private contract defense expertise) and the Muslims, as indicated by General Clark's discussion with the Bosniak leadership in 1994. During the war, American support to the Muslims and Croatians was an open secret among UN forces and NATO. The fact that the Clinton Administration chose to favor one side during the conflict was certainly acceptable, but the Administration was ultimately unwilling to expend American troops in obtaining peace, relying instead on Croat and Muslim surrogates.

The Clinton Administration's use of military force was tentative and unfocused in Bosnia and during the eight years of the Administration – failing to match political objectives with military forces. A statement by then American Ambassador to the United Nations Madeline Albright uttered in frustration at Colin Powell's observation that the US had no clear political objective in getting involved in Bosnia perhaps sums it up best, "What's the point of having this superb military that you're always talking about if we can't use it?" Powell reported that he thought he would have an aneurysm. Powell told Albright that,

"American GIs were not toy soldiers to be moved around on some sort of global game board."[114]

The American press consistently presented a pro-Muslim picture, downplaying Muslim and Croatian atrocities, while highlighting Serb atrocities (there were enough to go around). Examples include the series of reports produced by *CNN* in 1994 and *ABC*'s "The Peacekeeper: How the UN Failed in Bosnia" in 1995. Reports by both networks were selectively factual, describing atrocities and UN responses with a view that US intervention was necessary. In this, the press supported Administration objectives.

After the *Dayton Peace Accords* were initialed, the Yugoslav (Serbian) military attaché to Rome visited me in Naples for a briefing on how NATO forces would be deployed into Bosnia. At the conclusion of the briefing, the Yugoslav colonel asked, "why do Americans hate the Serbs?" I told him that the Muslims had done a better job of marketing themselves. For example, the Bosnian Muslim spokesman and UN envoy, Mohammed Sacirbey, was press friendly, on point, and spoke perfect American English (he holds dual Bosnian and US citizenship).[115] I told the colonel that when Serbian spokespersons met with the press, they had heavy accents, were evasive, and they tended to mislead and make allegations that were easily discredited. In short, when compared to the Bosnian Muslims, the Serbs were not media savvy.

The United Nations made themselves an easy target for press and Administration criticism by their inability to establish peace in Bosnia. Actions, such as the behavior of the Dutch battalion at Srebrenica, underscored an apparent adherence to a politically

---

[114] Colin Powell with Joseph E. Persico, *My American Journey* (New York: Ballantine Books, 1995). 561.

[115] Sacirbey was subsequently appointed Bosnian ambassador to the UN, then charged with embezzlement by the Bosnian government. He was accused of taking over $600,000 in 2000 alone (with over $2.5 million missing).

correct response to force. Organized to enforce a peace already agreed among warring factions UN "blue helmets" found themselves in over their heads. They were used to a culture of negotiation and passive restraint and generally could not transition to an environment demanding direct military action. By the end of the conflict, UN peacekeeping forces were largely discredited, at least with the American public.

## *Back to Iraq*

Following "Desert Storm", the cease fire agreement and United Nations Security Council resolutions called for restriction and elimination of Iraqi weapons. Weapons to be eliminated included tactical ballistic missiles with ranges in excess of 150 kilometers and WMD - weapons of mass destruction (chemical, biological and nuclear). Throughout the course of inspections over the next six years, Iraqi officials obstructed, deceived, delayed and blocked weapons inspectors – with a clear intent to conceal from inspectors the true nature of their ballistic missile and WMD programs. Iraqi actions to hide their work naturally led to speculation and suspicion that secret programs were still underway.

Part of the inspection process was regular surveillance overflights of selected areas by American U-2 reconnaissance aircraft. In fall 1997, Saddam blocked UN inspectors and threatened to shoot down U-2 aircraft. The US and UN demanded inspectors be allowed to return. Current and former Clinton Administration officials began to weigh in with the press. Former Clinton advisor George Stephanopoulos wrote an article in *Newsweek* magazine, in which he advocated assassination of Saddam as a practical solution to the ongoing Iraqi problem, while Secretary of Defense Cohen deflected Saddam's accusations that America was responsible for the death of Iraqi children due to international sanctions.[116] Investigations of the "Oil for Food" program later determined that money that should have gone to feed the starving children enriched Saddam and his friends in the international community.

In response, the United States, in coordination with Kuwait and allies from several nations, began moving forces to implement Operation "Desert Thunder" against Saddam in January 1998. The stated goal of the operation was to force Iraq to allow weapons inspectors' free access and to comply with UN Security Council mandates. Ground forces, including a brigade from the 3rd Infantry Division, were sent to Kuwait to prevent potential Iraqi efforts to re-invade the nation. One infantry brigade was already in country conducting an exercise before the beginning of "Desert Thunder". The US Navy took action to ensure the presence of at least two carrier battle groups in the area at all times (the *USS George Washington* was deployed to join the *USS Nimitz* battle group).

Predictably, Saddam backed down after meeting with UN General Secretary Kofi Annan in Baghdad. A crisis again ensued in early November 1998 as Saddam failed to live up to his promises and expelled the UN inspectors from the country, but he again agreed to allow inspectors back into Iraq and cooperate after President Clinton threatened a bombing campaign. Inspectors returned to Iraq on November 18, but by November 23, Saddam again refused to cooperate. President Clinton finally launched Operation "Desert Fox" on December 16, 1998, ordering air strikes against 100 targets suspected to be related to WMD programs. In an address to the nation, Clinton said,

"Saddam Hussein must not be allowed to threaten his neighbors or the world with nuclear arms, poison gas or

---

[116] Jamie McIntyre, "Cohen Blames Hussein for Infant Deaths," CNN, http://www.cnn.com/ALLPOLITICS/1997/12/01/email/cohen/, December 1, 1997. Accessed August 24, 2005

biological weapons," Clinton said. The Iraqi dictator has used these weapons against his neighbors and his own people, he said, and "left unchecked, Saddam Hussein will use these terrible weapons again."[117]

In the midst of the bombing campaign, the Iraqi government announced (ironically) that it would no longer cooperate with the UN inspectors. The operation lasted four days, ending on December 20, 1998, the first day of Ramadan. As the bombing campaign ended, three of the five members of the UN Security Council (Russia, France and China) called for an end to an oil embargo on Iraq, disbanding the UN inspection team and firing Richard Butler, the chief weapons inspector (these echoed Iraq's demands).[118] Although the US indicated that it would veto the proposal, the UN team was disbanded in December 1999 and Butler replaced by Hans Blix, who ultimately came to defend Saddam Hussein prior to and during the coalition invasion of Iraq in 2003.

"Desert Thunder" and "Desert Fox", as military operations were straightforward – deploy, deter invasion of Kuwait, and conduct limited attacks from a safe distance with the goal to reduce Saddam's weapons programs and force inspectors back into the country with some degree of cooperation. Placed in context, these military operations were in fact in the middle of two unfolding dramas – one in the Middle East and one in the United States. The story in the Middle East is of Saddam milking the UN for time and money, tweaking American noses and looking for chinks in coalition armor. In the United States, the confrontation with Saddam, along with actions against al Qaeda (covered in the next section), were played against a backdrop of President Clinton's impeachment scandal. Remarkable coincidences between international military action

---

[117] Linda D. Kozaryn, "Saddam Abused His Last Chance, Clinton Says", American Forces Information Service, updated January 14, 2003
[118] We now know, based on documents recovered following Iraqi Freedom, that Saddam intended to restart WMD programs once sanctions were lifted.

and impeachment activities (as depicted below) led many to conclude that President Clinton created a crisis to divert attention from his looming impeachment battle with Congress.

**Timeline – Actions against Iraq and Al Qaeda and the Scandal**

| Dates 1998 | Actions against Iraq and al Qaeda | Clinton Scandal |
|---|---|---|
| January 17 | | *Newsweek* Magazine decided not to run a story about the President and Monica Lewinsky. |
| January 21 | | Reports of the Lewinski affair appeared in the press. |
| January 27 | | The President denies having a relationship with Lewinski. |
| January - February | The President initiated Operation "Desert Thunder" to force Iraq to allow inspections. | |
| February 3 | Ayman al Zawahiri, a senior al Qaeda operative, reportedly visited Baghdad and met with the Iraqi Vice President to coordinate Iraqi and al Qaeda activities. | |
| February 17 | President Clinton's speech at the Pentagon on Iraq in which he condemned "an unholy axis of terrorists, drug traffickers and organized international criminals". | |
| February 28 | Bin Laden issued a *fatwa* against the US anticipating a US attack on Iraq. | |
| August 7 | Terrorists attacked two US embassies in Africa. Al Qaeda is suspected. | |
| August 17 | | President Clinton testified before a grand jury, then went on national television to admit an affair with Monica Lewinski. |
| August 20 | | The President submits a DNA sample. |
| August 21 | The US launched attacks | |

| Dates 1998 | Actions against Iraq and al Qaeda | Clinton Scandal |
|---|---|---|
| | against a pharmaceutical factory believed to be making chemical weapons materials, with ties to Iraq and al Qaeda; and an attack against terrorist training camps in Afghanistan. | |
| December 16 | The President launched Operation "Desert Fox" against Iraq. | |
| December 19 | | The House of Representatives passed two articles of impeachment. |
| December 20 | Operation "Desert Fox" ended. | |

A closer look at the events in Iraq and with Al Qaeda immediately before and during the Lewinski scandal indicates that the President was really in a "no win" situation. Perhaps Saddam and bin Laden took advantage of the scandal to some extent after it began, but the immediate crisis with weapons inspectors in Iraq began before the Lewinski affair broke. Al Qaeda's response appears to be tied to US intervention in Iraq (per bin Laden's *fatwa* issued in February 1998 – but more on that later). The President responded to each Iraqi and Al Qaeda development with limited (perhaps too limited) force.

Throughout President Clinton's tenure in office, he was vulnerable to critical attacks regarding his use of the military. Coincidences such as those listed above served to amplify such criticism.

## The Clinton Administration and Al Qaeda

One of the unintended consequences of the Soviet invasion of Afghanistan in 1979 was the creation of a *jihad* – a holy war against the Soviets by Muslims from around the world. One young Saudi that went to fight the Soviets was Osama bin Laden (also spelled Usama bin Ladin). Six foot, five inches tall, he stood out among his fellow fighters, not only because of his height and athletic ability, but also because of his family's enormous wealth. Bin Laden contributed heavily to the war and was involved in the development of a worldwide financial support network called the "Golden Chain" organized by Arab governments and financiers. The Golden Chain was enhanced by direct governmental funding of the Afghan rebels, including military aid from the United States. Fighters were recruited in mosques, schools and other gathering places.

Following the Soviet withdrawal from Afghanistan in 1988, bin Laden worked to maintain the infrastructure established during the war, for use in future holy wars. He quickly rose to the top of this new base or foundation, al Qaeda.

This organization's structure included as its operating arms an intelligence component, a military committee, a financial committee, a political committee, and a committee in charge of media affairs and propaganda. It also had an Advisory Council (*Shura*) made up of Bin Laden's inner circle.[119]

In 1989, a governmental leader in Sudan invited bin Laden to move his organization there. The shift to Sudan began while bin Laden moved back to Saudi Arabia in 1990. When Iraq invaded Kuwait, bin Laden approached the Saudi government about using al Qaeda to create a *jihad* to drive the Iraqis out of Kuwait. Instead, the Saudi government joined the US led coalition. Bin Laden criticized the Saudi decision, was repressed and fled to Sudan in 1991. While in Sudan, bin Laden established widespread, complex business operations, which included: a "service" organization in Zagreb (Croatia); an office of the Benevolence International Foundation in Sarajevo, established to support Bosnian Muslims; an operation that supported rebels in Chechnya; an operation to provide equipment

---

[119] *The 9/11 Commission Report,* (Washington DC: US Government Printing Office, undated), 56.

and training the Abu Sayyaf Brigade in the Philippines (the organization which took Martin and Gracia Burnham prisoner in May 2001); and non-governmental "charity" organizations in various locations.[120]

In 1992, al Qaeda issued a *fatwa* for a *jihad* to remove Western presence (particularly the United States) from Islamic nations. Also in 1992, al Qaeda began to work with Somali warlords against US troops. They sent several trainers to Somalia, including their most senior weapons experts, who later boasted about their assistance in shooting down the Blackhawk helicopters during "Blackhawk Down" in October 1993. They took credit for forcing the Americans out of Somalia in 1994. In 1995, al Qaeda shipped explosives to Saudi Arabia used in a car bomb attack that killed five Americans and two Indians. Al Qaeda also apparently played a support role in the Iranian backed attack that killed 19 and wounded 372 Americans at Khobar Towers in Dhaharn. Bin Laden was at least peripherally involved in the first (1993) attack on the World Trade Center in New York.

Bin Laden began reaching out to other anti-American elements in the Islamic world, including Iran and Iraq. In 1991 or 1992, meetings between al Qaeda and Iranian representatives led to informal agreements regarding training and cooperation in attacks against the United States. Al Qaeda leaders went to Iran, then to the Bekaa Valley in Lebanon in 1993 for explosives, intelligence and security training. As indicated above, the Khobar tower bombings indicate some degree of cooperation between Iran and al Qaeda during the 1990's.

Al Qaeda's relations with Iraq had a rocky start.[121] Hussein was a secular Ba'ath Party ruler focused on Arab nationalism,

---

[120] Ibid., 58.

[121] Information regarding relationships between Iraq and al Qaeda is taken, in part, from a *Weekly Standard* article written by Stephen F. Hayes in the November 24, 2003 issue. The article is based on a classified memo written by Undersecretary Douglas Feith to the Senate

not Islamic revolution – however, he was willing to don the mantle of an Islamic champion when convenient. Bin Laden opposed the Iraqi invasion of Kuwait and enlisted the support of anti-Saddam elements in Iraq's Kurdistan. But bin Laden's Sudanese host, al-Turabi, who had a close relationship with Iraq, undertook to settle disagreements between bin Laden and Hussein. In 1992, Al-Turabi organized a meeting between the Iraqi intelligence deputy director Farup Hujanzi and senior al Qaeda leader Ayman al Zawahiri in Sudan. Meetings between these organizations continued in Sudan until 1995. In 1993, bin Laden and Saddam reached an agreement that al Qaeda would no longer support anti-Saddam activities. Iraq provided bomb-making training to al Qaeda from Brigadier Salim al-Ahmed, Iraq's senior explosives expert, who visited al Qaeda in Sudan in 1995 and 1996 along with the director of Iraqi intelligence, Mani abd-al-Rashid al-Tikriti. Activity between Iraq and al Qaeda increased during early 1998 and again in December 1998, as Saddam faced US pressure over UN weapons inspectors. Al Zqwahiri went to Baghdad and visited with the Iraqi vice-president on February 3, 1998 to arrange coordination to establish training camps in Iraq.[122] A few days later, on February 28, 1998, bin Laden issued his now famous *fatwa*, declaring war on the United States based the impending US led actions against Iraq. The text of this *fatwa* included:

> The ruling to kill the Americans and their allies – civilians and military – is an individual duty for every Muslim who can do it in any country in which it is possible to do it, in order to liberate the al-Aqsa Mosque and the holy mosque (Mecca) from their grip, and in order for their armies to move out of all of the lands of Islam, defeated and unable to threaten any Muslim. This is in accordance with the words of Almighty God, "and fight the pagans all together as they

---

Intelligence Committee. The memo summarizes al Qaeda and Iraqi contacts in 50 separate points.

[122] Iraqi intelligence documents uncovered after the 2003 US led invasion, revealed Iraqi plans to fund al Qaeda trips to Iraq to coordinate future operations.

fight you all together," and "fight them until there is no more tumult or oppression, and there prevail justice and faith in God."[123]

By 1995, bin Laden's days in Sudan were numbered. Outside pressure, from the US, the United Nations, and even terrorist friendly nations in the region including Syria and Libya, caused the Sudanese government to reconsider their arrangements with al Qaeda. Also, Sudan had been placed on the US State Department list of states sponsoring terrorism, and they wanted off. Financial pressures resulted in bin Laden running short of funds, causing some key defections among his membership. Sudan began to look for places to send bin Laden and his organization. In October 1994, they had turned "Carlos the Jackal" over to the French, and essentially wanted to do the same thing with bin Laden. According to Mansoor Ijaz, an American Muslim and investment banker who later coauthored the blueprint for the ceasefire agreement in Kashmir in 2000, he became a go-between for the Clinton Administration and government of Sudan in 1996, trying to figure out what to do with bin Laden. On March 8, 1996, the Sudanese Defense Minister met with David Shinn of the CIA to tell him that the Sudanese government was willing to arrest bin Laden and turn him over to the US. Separately, and at about the same time, Ijaz relayed to Clinton National Security Advisor "Sandy" Berger and President Clinton that Sudan was willing to arrest and turn bin Laden over to American authorities or any government the United States would designate. Barring that, the Sudanese offered to keep bin Laden in Sudan and monitor his activities, but the US continued to place pressure on Sudan to force him out. So in May 1996, bin Laden went back to Afghanistan, taking key lieutenants al Zawahiri and Wadih El-Hage (now serving a life sentence in the US for his involvement in the 1998 bombings of US embassies in Tanzania and Kenya). At the time

---

[123] Bin Laden, Al-Zawahiri, and Rifa'I Taha, "To Kill Americans Everywhere" published by *Al Quds al'Arabi*, London, February 28, 1998

136

of Sudan's offer, a US counterterrorism official reportedly said, "I really cared about one thing, and that was getting him out of Sudan."[124]

From fall 1996 until shortly before September 2001, Sudan offered to provide information on al Qaeda operatives, based on dossiers they had assembled over several years, and the FBI wished to obtain this information, but the State Department objected. Ijaz reported that he was approached again in 2000 (three months before the *USS Cole* attack) by an Arab country willing to extradite bin Laden to the US, but Clinton Administration officials mishandled the offer and bin Laden remained free.[125]

The Clinton Administration offered various reasons for not taking up Sudan's offer to turn bin Laden over. First, officials denied the offer was made. They later objected that they did not believe the Sudanese were serious about arresting bin Laden and turning him over (ignoring Sudanese complicity in turning over Carlos to the French). The last argument was that they did not want the responsibility. National Security Advisor Sandy Burger said, "The FBI did not believe we had enough evidence to indict bin Laden at that time and therefore opposed bringing him to the United States."[126]

Throughout the 1990's, al Qaeda was suspected or claimed involvement in several terrorist attacks against Americans and US interests. Three bombings were targeted against US troops in Aden and Yemen in 1992 with no US casualties; however one

---

[124] Richard Miniter, "Sudan's Angle: How Clinton Passed Up an Opportunity to Stop Osama bin Laden", *Wall Street Journal*, October 8, 2001.

[125] Mansoor Ijaz, "Clinton Let Bin Laden Slip Away and Metastasize", *Los Angeles Times*, December 5, 2001.

[126] Kathryn Jean Lopez, interview with Richard Miniter, "Clinton's Loss*", National Review On-Line*, September 11, 2003. www.nationalreview.com/interrogatory/interrogatory091103b.asp. Accessed October 21, 2005.

Austrian tourist and a Yemeni died. Al Qaeda was most certainly indirectly involved in aiding Aidid's attack against "Task Force Ranger" in Somalia in 1993 (resulting in the "Battle of Mogadishu"). In November 1995, al Qaeda was probably involved in the Riyadh bombing of a US military facility (killing five Americans and two Indians), and provided some assistance in the 1996 Khobar Towers bombing. Both the Riyadh and Khobar Towers attacks are usually attributed to Hezbullah as the primary attacking organization. Amidst the ongoing crisis in Iraq over the UN arms inspectors, Al Qaeda coordinated the bombings of US embassies in Kenya and Tanzania in August 1998, killing more than 200 people and injuring 5,000 others. Al Qaeda attempted to bomb the Los Angeles International Airport during the millennium holiday, but the bomber (Ahmed Ressam) was caught at the Canadian border trying to enter the United States. An attempt to attack the *USS The Sullivans* in January 2000 failed due to technical reasons, but an attack on the *USS Cole* in October 2000 was successful, killing 17 sailors. One report indicated that a total of 59 Americans were killed by al Qaeda from 1992 to 2000.

In November 1998, the United States issued an indictment against Osama bin Laden, claiming that he operated a terror network called "al Qaeda". In this and subsequent indictments, the Government alleged that bin Laden formed al Qaeda in 1989 with the intent to oppose non-Islamic governments with violence, to drive US armed forces out of Saudi Arabia and Somalia by violence, that he operated a council (*Shura*) to coordinate terrorists activities (thus, a criminal conspiracy), and that he cooperated with other known terrorist organizations or nations (including Sudan, Iraq and Syria).

In 1996, President Clinton signed a secret order that authorized the CIA to use any and all means to destroy al Qaeda. In August 1996 (after the Khobar Towers bombing), a secret grand jury investigation began in New York. In June 1998, US and Albanian security personnel raided terrorist cells with ties to bin Laden in Albania, resulting in four arrests and the seizing of computers and documents. Also in June 1998, the grand jury issued a sealed indictment (which was superseded by the November 1998 indictment summarized above). After the embassy bombings in August 1998, the President authorized retaliatory strikes against the pharmaceutical factory and Afghan training camps (discussed earlier). In 1999 and 2000, the President deferred or cancelled proposed strikes against bin Laden himself.

After al Qaeda's attack on the *USS Cole*, a meeting took place between counterterrorism expert Richard Clarke along with Michael Sheehan (the State Department counterterrorism coordinator) and Defense Secretary Cohen, Director of Central Intelligence Tenet, Secretary of State Albright, and Attorney General Reno to discuss the US response to the attack. Essentially, the assembled group expressed concern about possible violations of international law and not enough provocation for a military action (except Clarke, who pushed for a military strike). Apparently, Michael Sheehan was surprised in particular by Cohen's reaction, and told Clarke afterward, "What's it going to take to get them to hit al Qaeda in Afghanistan? Does al Qaeda have to attack the Pentagon?"[127]

The Clinton Administration's response to the al Qaeda threat was to take a law enforcement, rather than a military view. Although bin Laden had declared war on the United States in February 1998, the President didn't see the conflict as a war, but quite literally as a police action. In retrospect, it is easy to place blame on the President and his advisors – they were trying to work within an established framework of legal precedence.

## *The Kosovo Campaign*

Like Bosnia, conflict in Kosovo can be traced back centuries. In spite of the violent nature of the region, Yugoslav communist dictator Tito was able to suppress nationalistic tendencies and maintain a semblance of cooperation. Tito,

---

[127] Lopez, "Clinton's Loss".

recognizing that nationalism would tear apart his nation, put policies into place to dilute nationalism by trying to spread economic loads throughout the nation and using the Communist Party as a central organizing authority. In Kosovo, two ethnic groups vied for control – the Serbs (who eventually dominated what was left of Yugoslavia) and the ethnic Albanians, who were predominantly Muslim.

When Tito died in 1980, underground nationalistic movements began to emerge. In 1989, Serbian communist leader Slobodan Milosevic declared a state of emergency in Kosovo and in 1990 he curtailed the republic's autonomy within Yugoslavia – charging that the rights of Serbs in Kosovo were being violated. Kosovo's assembly and government were disbanded, and state-employed ethnic Albanians were replaced with Serbs. Official use of the Albanian language was banned in print and broadcast journalism. Unemployment soared and as many as 1/3 of adult Albanian males went abroad looking for work. The Democratic League of Kosovo emerged as a political entity, led by a writer, Ibrahim Rugova. A shadow assembly and government were established and boycotts of Yugoslav products, taxes, the draft, etc. developed.

Many Albanians considered armed rebellion their only viable option. In 1996, the Kosovo Liberation Army (KLA) appeared and began a campaign to provoke Serbian security forces into reprisals which, in theory, would promote support for the KLA and perhaps cause NATO to get involved (as it did in Bosnia). The US response in 1997-1998 was to declare the KLA a terrorist organization (with some justification) and try to work through a "Contact Group" – composed of Britain, France, Germany, Italy, Russia and the United States – to resolve issues in Kosovo. In late 1997, the Albanian (not to be confused with Kosovo) government collapsed and arms depots were raided with large amounts of weapons ending up in the hands of the KLA. Serbs responded with the deployment of paramilitary police and an armed Serb militia, led by "Arkan"[128] a Serbian gangster, bank robber, and leader of "Arkan's Tigers" during the Bosnian War. The very presence of Arkan operating in the area led to suspicion of atrocities. By 1998, hundreds had been killed and hundreds of thousands of people displaced. Albanian refugees fled to neighboring Macedonia, threatening to upset that country with ethnic strife between Macedonians and Albanians – a situation that could draw in the neighboring countries of Serbia, Albania, Greece and Bulgaria. Finally, NATO, the European Union and the Organization for Security and Cooperation in Europe (OSCE) decided that something had to be done. OCSE took the lead by deploying unarmed monitors after a cease fire was declared in October 1998. This succeeded only in providing a ready supply of hostages (as in Bosnia four years earlier – they never learn). Fighting resumed in December.

On January 8 and 10, 1999, the KLA attacked Serbian police in the vicinity of a town named Racak, resulting in several casualties. Serbs cordoned the area and rumors of a massacre began circulating. OSCE monitors were able to get into the area on January 16 and found about 40 bodies in and around the town. The OSCE declared a massacre had occurred before investigating whether the individuals had died as a result of fighting (as KLA members); were villagers massacred by Serb police; or, as alleged later by French journalists traveling with the Serb police, the bodies were planted by the KLA. Regardless of the cause of death, Racak generated NATO action. NATO warned both sides to cease combat operations or suffer the consequences of air strikes, and demanded that Kosovo be returned to the semi-autonomous status they enjoyed under Tito,

---

[128] "Arkan" was the *nom de guerre* for Zeljko Raznatovic (1952-2000), who was a bank robber, mobster, hit man, politician and mercenary. He also sold ice cream. He was seen as a folk hero, sort of a modern day Robin Hood, to many Serbs. His paramilitary "Arkan's Tigers" was a force of 10,000 well trained Serbian militia who fought in virtually every key battle during the Bosnian War. Arkan was assassinated in the lobby of the Intercontinental Hotel in Belgrade on January 15, 2000 by a Serbian policeman on sick leave.

plus a democratic government (called by the Contact Group, "Status Quo Plus"). NATO Secretary General Javier Solana led talks in February 1999 at Rambouillet, near Paris, but results were inconclusive. Both sides rejected Status Quo Plus – ethnic Albanians wanted an independent Kosovo, while the Yugoslav (Serb) government wanted no autonomy at all for Kosovo. In the end, the Albanian, American and British delegations signed the *Rambouillet Accords* while the Serbs and Russians refused.

OCSE observers left in March 1999. NATO bombing began on March 24 to force the Serbs to agree to the Accords. Bombing continued until June 10. A NATO spokesman summarized their goals: "Serbs out, peacekeepers in, refugees back." NATO seriously underestimated Milosevic's will to resist. The intensity of airstrikes were well below those used during "Desert Storm", and the lack of NATO troops on the ground ensured intensified fighting between the warring factions during the bombing campaign. In April, NATO reported that 850,000 people (mostly Albanians) had been displaced. Airstrikes began against strategic targets but moved to individual tactical targets, such as tanks – but each target had to be agreed to by all 19 NATO nations (a situation that was never contemplated during "Deliberate Force" in Bosnia four years earlier). Two bombing errors caused an international uproar. In one case, fleeing Albanian refugees were bombed (thought to be a Serb convoy) and 50 people were killed. The second case was the mistaken bombing of the Chinese Embassy in Belgrade (due, of all things, to an incorrect street address). Ironically, the Russians intervened to resolve the conflict by putting pressure on Milosevic to back off and telling him that they would not support his continued resistance.

Immediately after the cease fire, NATO claimed that the bombing was extremely effective. However, post-strike analysis indicated that only 13 tanks or armored vehicles were destroyed while most of the precision munitions hit Serbian dummy vehicles. Yugoslav forces kept NATO aircraft above 15,000 feet by the threat of their air defense system, although they never turned their systems on.  Criticism of American involvement in the bombing campaign came from both sides.  Conservatives pointed out that no clear political goals were set, nor were US national interests involved.  Liberals accused the US government of imperialism.

The actual status of Kosovo remains unresolved.  It is still formally a part of Yugoslavia, but the central government has little control over Kosovo.  Albanians continue to demand independence, so the threat of instability remains.

## Conclusion – America's Wars of the 1990's

During the early years of the Clinton Administration, then Defense Secretary Les Aspin discarded the "Powell Doctrine" as a test for the use of military force before placing troops in harm's way.

So, what is the "Powell Doctrine"?  After the Marine barracks were attacked in Beirut in 1983, then Secretary of Defense Casper Weinberger made a speech at the National Press Club on November 28, 1984, in which he articulated six tests that should be met before US troops are committed to combat. They are:

- Is a vital US interest at stake?
- Will we commit sufficient resources to win?
- Are the objectives clearly defined?
- Will we sustain the commitment?
- Is there reasonable expectation that the public and Congress will support the operation?
- Have we exhausted our other options?

In truth, these questions reach well beyond the use of Marines in Lebanon to the lessons of Vietnam.  The *Washington Post* dubbed the six questions the "Weinberger Doctrine".  Because of Colin Powell's application of these questions while he was Chairman of the Joint Chiefs, they became associated with him.

Secretary Aspin said that the "Powell Doctrine" was too restrictive – an all or nothing decision with no flexibility. For military professionals, the "Powell Doctrine" made a lot of sense, particularly to those who were young officers during Vietnam. In a view hauntingly similar to the Kennedy Administration's approach that led to US involvement in Vietnam, Aspin indicated that limited warfare would be the way of the future and overwhelming combat power would no longer be needed. What the Clinton Administration (and presumably Secretary Aspin) proposed instead was a doctrine of "assertive multilateralism" – the idea that military operations would be conducted only through multilateral organizations such as the United Nations or NATO. The first application of this approach resulted in the Battle of Mogadishu, and the deaths of 18 soldiers, with the US leaving the region in defeat. Ironically, Mogadishu failed, in part, because the Administration ignored their own doctrine of multilateralism in cutting the UN commander that owned the firepower (the Pakistanis) in Somalia out of the equation, until he was needed to help rescue an under-resourced American force. Because of Somalia, Clinton signed Presidential Decision Directive (PDD) 25 that established criteria for commitment of force – a document the Administration also promptly ignored in Bosnia and Macedonia.

Beyond the issue of when and how to commit military power, a pattern of international caution and indecisiveness by the Clinton Administration suggested to friends and enemies that the US would not seriously respond to an attack on Americans or US interests. A first glimpse was revealed in Mogadishu and reinforced in Bosnia[129] and confirmed by Clinton's tepid

---

[129] The culture of "force protection" was so strong in Bosnia after US troops entered as part of the peace implementation force, that other nations called US troops "Ninja Turtles", a derisive description of the fact that US troops were required to travel in herds of vehicles wearing helmets and flack vests as if they were in full combat, while other

responses to al Qaeda's bombing of US embassies in Africa in 1998 and attack on the *USS Cole*. Bin Laden came to expect limited, and to him, acceptable responses to his attacks. Some have suggested that this expectation convinced him that a major attack on the United States would force a massive US withdrawal from the Middle East – a larger version of the withdrawal from Somalia in 1994.

Finally, the Clinton Administration always viewed the conflict with al Qaeda as a law enforcement issue. Events underscore that approach and reveal how "in the box" legal thinking created opportunities for al Qaeda and others to operate successfully during the 1990's

The first World Trade Center bombing occurred in 1993. In an article, written in 1995 (after the first bombing but well before September 11) Laurie Mylorie wrote,

> The details of the World Trade Center case are chilling. From the outset, the Justice Department refused to share key information with the national security agencies. The government had two sets of relevant information – foreign intelligence, gathered by the CIA from watching terrorist states such as Iran and Iraq, and evidence gathered by the FBI largely within the United States for use in the trial. The FBI flatly told the national security bureaucracies that there was "no evidence" of state sponsorship in the World Trade Center bombing. When the national security agencies asked to see the evidence themselves, the FBI replied, "No, this is a criminal matter. We're handling it." Thus, all the national security agencies had available to decide the question of state sponsorship was foreign intelligence they themselves had collected.[130]

---

nation's troops wore soft hats, carried only side arms and traveled in groups of two.
[130] Laurie Mylroie, "The World Trade Center Bomb: Who is Ramzi Yousef? And Why it Matters", *The National Interest*, Winter 1995/96

A wall existed between intelligence and law enforcement organizations. Law enforcement officials would not accept information from intelligence agencies for fear that such information would be inadmissible in court and taint evidence for criminal trial. In addition, law enforcement agencies weren't looking for state sponsored terrorism – they sought to prosecute individuals, such as Ramzi Yousef, the first World Trade Center bomber.

The wall of separation between law enforcement and intelligence agencies was strengthened by a memo written by former Clinton Deputy Attorney General Jamie Gorelick (later a member of the 9-11 Commission), in which she addressed the conduct of investigations surrounding the first World Trade Center bombing. In the memo, Ms. Gorelick stated her purpose was to:

> . . . establish a set of instructions that will clearly separate the counterintelligence investigation from the more limited, but continued, criminal investigations. These procedures, which go beyond what is legally required, will prevent any risk of creating an unwarranted appearance that FISA (Foreign Intelligence Surveillance Act) is being used to avoid procedural safeguards which would apply in a criminal investigation.[131]

When Osama bin Laden was offered up by the Sudanese government, the US did not take him into custody because of a lack of evidence that he had committed criminal acts. Ironically, the wall of separation between intelligence and law enforcement did not allow a case to be built against bin Laden until the grand jury indictments in June and November 1998.

---

[131] Jamie S. Gorelick, "Instructions on Separation of Certain Foreign Counterintelligence and Criminal Investigations," Office of the Deputy Attorney General, undated, declassified on April 10, 2004.

Counterintelligence operators in the super-classified Able Danger program may have identified cells associated with the future September 11 bombings more than a year before the attack, but were prevented from passing that information to the FBI because of the wall of separation.

## Chapter Seven

# The "War on Terror"

*"States like these, and their terrorist allies, constitute and axis of evil, arming to threaten the peace of the world. By seeking weapons of mass destruction, these regimes pose a grave and growing danger. They could provide these arms to terrorists, giving them the means to match their hatred. They could attack our allies or attempt to blackmail the United States. In any of these cases, the price of indifference would be catastrophic."*

George W. Bush
2002 State of the Union Address
(Referring to Iran, Iraq and North Korea)

September 11, 2001 is one of those days that people remember. Like the day that Pearl Harbor was bombed, that Franklin Roosevelt died, that John Kennedy was shot, or that the Challenger exploded, people tend to recall exactly where they were; what they were doing; what they smelled, saw, or heard; and the emotions they experienced when they first heard or saw the news.

September 11 (9-11) began a new era in American history, the "War on Terror". This chapter will briefly review actions taken immediately after 9-11, combat in Afghanistan and combat in Iraq until the cessation of major hostilities in 2003.

## *Attack on America*

Al Qaeda operatives selected for the 9-11 attacks began arriving in the US in early 2000. The first arrivals trained as pilots primarily in Florida, Oklahoma and Arizona. Meanwhile, bin Laden personally selected the "muscle" (men that stormed and took control of the planes) between the summer of 2000 and April 2001. Muscle hijackers traveled to the United States between April and June 2001, several of them transiting through Iran, with the assistance of Iranian security, to maintain clean passports (no visa stamps) in order to disguise their transit. During the summer of 2001, the pilot terrorists honed their flight skills by taking additional instruction, spending time in simulators and renting light aircraft to recon their flight routes. Mohammed Atta, the al Qaeda tactical leader of the attack, selected the attack date by mid August and passed the date along to his controller, Khalid Sheikh Mohammed (KSM). Bin Laden approved the targets: the World Trade Center, Pentagon, US Capitol and the White House (his personal priority target).

Construction started on the World Trade Center complex in 1966, and with the first tenants occupying offices in 1970. The Twin Towers, the centerpiece of the multi-building complex, dominated the New York skyline, rising to 110 stories each, with upwards of 50,000 people occupying workspace. The World Trade Center had been bombed before, in 1993 by a team including Ramzi Yousef, KSM's nephew.

At 8:46 AM hijackers flew American Airlines Flight 11 into an area between the $93^{rd}$ and $99^{th}$ floors of the North Tower. At 9:03 AM, United Airlines Flight 175 hit the South Tower between the $77^{th}$ and $85^{th}$ floors. At 9:58, the South Tower collapsed in approximately 10 seconds, followed by the collapse of the North Tower at 10:28. At 10:03, United Flight 93 crashed into a field in Pennsylvania. In Virginia, at 9:37, American Airlines Flight 77 slammed into the west wall of the Pentagon traveling at approximately 530 miles per hour.

In Manhattan, 25 buildings were damaged; four subway stations destroyed or badly damaged, communications systems knocked out (due to destruction of communications towers). One section of the Pentagon collapsed. The human toll was devastating. A total of 265 people were killed on the four aircraft. Three hundred forty three New York fireman, 23 New York City policemen and 37 Port Authority policemen were killed. One hundred twenty five civilian and military personnel were killed at the Pentagon. Total approximate dead for the day was 2,985.

## *Declaration – War on Terror*

Historian Victor Davis Hanson frames the background of anti-American terrorism within a context of hatred in search of an ideology. He writes,

> Contrary to popular opinion, there has not been a single standard doctrine of hatred in the Middle East. Radical Islam is just the most recent brand of many successive pathologies, not necessarily any more embraced by a billion people than Hitler's Nazism was characteristic of the entire West.

> In the 1940s the raging-ism in the Middle East was anti-Semitic secular fascism, copycatting Hitler and Mussolini – who seemed by 1942 ascendant and victorious.

> Between the 1950s and 1970s Soviet-style atheistic Ba'athism and tribal Pan-Arabism were deemed the waves of the future and unstoppable.

> By the 1980s Islamism was the new antidote for the old bacillus of failure and inadequacy.

> Each time an –ism was defeated, it was only to be followed by another – as it always is in the absence of free markets and constitutional government.

> Saddam started out as a pro-Soviet communist puppet, then fancied himself a fascistic dictator and pan-Arabist nationalist, and ended up building mosques, always in search of the most resonant strain of hatred. Arafat was once a left-wing atheistic thug. When the Soviet Union waned, he dropped the boutique socialism, and became a South-American-style caudillo. At the end of his days, he too got

religion as the Arab Street turned to fundamentalism and Hamas threatened to eat away at his support.[132]

In addressing the threat of terrorism, the Bush Administration evolved what is known as the "Bush Doctrine". Immediately after the 9-11 attacks, the Bush Doctrine was simply that the US would make no distinction between the terrorists and those who harbor them. The invasion of Afghanistan, destruction of the Taliban and dismantling of al Qaeda were immediate results of the doctrine. Over time, however, the Bush Doctrine developed into a set of policies articulated by President Bush at the 2002 commencement ceremony at West Point.[133] The expanded doctrine includes four points:

- Preemption – The US and its allies have the right to conduct preemptive attacks to prevent terror strikes. The President's speech at West Point, developed over a period of weeks before, is the first mention of "preemption" as a doctrinal element of the "War on Terror".

- Unilateralism – The US has the right to pursue unilateral military action in the event that multi-lateral solutions are unattainable.

- Strength beyond challenge – The US will maintain its status as the sole superpower.

- Extending democracy – Bush said at West Point, "America has no empire to extend or utopia to establish. We wish for others only what we wish for ourselves – safety from

---

[132] Victor Davis Hanson, "Reformation or Civil War?" *National Review Online*, July 29, 2005.
[133] George W. Bush, "Remarks by the President at 2002 Graduation Exercise of the United States Military Academy West Point, New York", http://www.whitehouse.gov/news/releases/2002/06/20020601-3.html. Accessed August 23, 2005.

violence, the rewards of liberty, and the hope for a better life."

Prior to the Bush Doctrine, American foreign policy was an extension of the Cold War ideas of deterrence (based on George Kennan's containment concept)[134] and multilateralism. Individuals within the Bush Administration, when surveying the new threat, suggested that deterrence, containment and multilateralism only work with a Western oriented, rationally thinking enemy (a description that included the Soviet Union) but not the current crop of Middle Eastern terrorists.

The Bush Doctrine implemented the Administration's global "War on Terror" (also called by Defense Secretary Rumsfeld the "global struggle against violent extremism"). Bush's view was that conflict with al Qaeda and similar state and non-state sponsored terrorism was a war, and should be treated as a war. Critics, such as those with the former Clinton Administration, took the view that the struggle was a law enforcement issue, not military combat. Consequently, criticism was framed in that context – that constitutional rights of non-citizens were being violated, that detainees were not given due process, that the rights of citizens were being curtailed by legislation such as the Patriot Act, and that evidence of Saddam's involvement in 9-11 was faint at best. In short, liberal critics wished to gather evidence, indict and convict while the Bush Administration wished to destroy terrorist infrastructure and prevent new attacks.

## *Afghanistan*

In the vacuum of Soviet withdrawal from Afghanistan, warlords vied for power. One group, the Taliban, a

---

[134] The notable exception to the Cold War era foreign policy trend was the Reagan Doctrine. However, the president after Reagan, George H. W. Bush, generally returned to foreign policy precedents of previous presidents, not to follow the line taken by Reagan.

fundamentalist Islamic group backed by at least some in the government of Pakistan, began a military conquest of the country, seizing control of the capital city, Kabul in September 1996. As Afghani warlords began to defect to the Taliban, Pakistan recognized them as the official government of Afghanistan on May 25, 1997 with Saudi Arabia following suit the next day. The United Arab Emirates became the third and final country to recognize the Taliban. Beginning in 1997, the Saudi's sent approximately $2 million a year in aid to the Taliban.

Once the Taliban assumed power, they implemented Islamic law as the law of the land. Accordingly, they banned all forms of television, music, sports, and the wearing of white shoes (the Taliban color) was forbidden. Men were required to wear their beards at a designated length. Women were required to wear *burqas* in public, were restricted in educational opportunities and barred from holding jobs. Perplexed by the Western reaction to their treatment of women, the Taliban Religion Minister asked the *New York Times* "Why is there such concern about women? Bread costs too much. There is no work. Even boys are not going to school. And yet all I hear about are women. Where was the world when men here were violating any woman they wanted?"

Osama bin Laden moved to Afghanistan from the Sudan in 1996 because of intense international pressure on the government of Sudan. He was able to develop a close, cooperative arrangement with the Taliban when they came to power shortly after his arrival. For example, al Qaeda trained organizations were integrated into the Taliban Afghani army between 1996 and 2001 while the Taliban provided safe haven for al Qaeda training camps. In August 1998, the Clinton Administration fired cruise missiles at suspected terrorist training camps in retaliation for the al Qaeda bombings of two US embassies in Africa. The attacks did very little damage on the ground.

After 9-11, Saudi Arabia and the United Arab Emirates withdrew diplomatic recognition, leaving Pakistan as the only nation officially supporting the Taliban. President George W. Bush issued an ultimatum to the Taliban, which included: deliver al Qaeda leaders in Afghanistan to the US; release all imprisoned foreign nationals (including Americans); protect foreign journalists, diplomats and aid workers; close terrorist training camps in Afghanistan and give full access to camps to ensure they were closed. The Taliban, at first, demanded proof of al Qaeda involvement in 9-11, but later through their embassy in Pakistan, offered to extradite bin Laden to a neutral country. Bush believed they were insincere in their offer. The UN Security Council passed a resolution on September 18, 2001 that echoed many of Bush's demands.

The "Northern Alliance" of Afghani warlords on which the United States would eventually depend to help win the ground war was made up of factions that had formerly controlled the country before the Taliban. When the Taliban took control of Afghanistan, they were able to defeat future Northern Alliance factions due to divisions caused by their own vicious infighting and tribal warfare. As the Northern Alliance emerged as a viable force, one of the key leaders, Ahmed Shah Massoud was assassinated on September 9, 2001 (two days before 9-11) by al Qaeda operatives posing as journalists. Recognized by al Qaeda as a key organizing figure among the Taliban's enemies, Massoud had been the subject of a novel by Ken Follett, *Lie Down with Lions*, about the Soviet invasion of Afghanistan.

As American military planners began to turn their attention to Afghanistan, "talking heads" on the Sunday morning talk show circuit repeated predictions of American failure based on the Soviet experience in Afghanistan, the coming winter in the brutal Afghan highlands, and the ubiquitous predictions of another "Vietnam".

US and British Special Forces infiltrated into Afghanistan to link up with Northern Alliance military units before the start of active combat. The coalition bombing campaign started on October 7, 2001 against al Qaeda training camps and Taliban (Afghani) air defense systems. Pundits had predicted severe losses of US aircraft, expecting extensive use of left-over Stinger missiles the United States provided to the *mujahedin* during the Soviet-Afghan war – but no Stingers were reportedly used by the Taliban during the campaign. Once the Taliban air defenses were destroyed or suppressed, air attacks shifted to destroy the Taliban command and control capabilities. Northern Alliance units, however, made little initial headway against the Taliban in the north, and they requested additional attention to enemy units on their front. At about that time, critics in the US accused military leaders of losing their way and Pakistani fighters started pouring across the border to help the Taliban.

Toward the end of October 2001, as tactical bombing of Taliban units opposing the Northern Alliance began to have an affect, 100 US Army Rangers raided deep into enemy territory to the Taliban spiritual home at Kandahar. The Rangers gathered intelligence data and left behind flyers entitled "Freedom Endures" that included a photograph of firefighters raising the American flag over the wreckage of the World Trade Center.

At the beginning of November, 2001, Taliban front lines experienced 15,000 pound "daisy cutter" bombs and devastatingly precise strikes from AC-130 gunships called in by Special Forces operators with the Northern Alliance.[135] Taliban forces crumbled under the onslaught by November 2. Throughout the remainder of Taliban held Afghanistan, al Qaeda fighters began to assume control of local security as Taliban forces began to disintegrate.

On November 9, Northern Alliance units attacked the northern provincial capital of Mazar-e-Sharif. The Taliban attempted to defend the Chesmay-e-Safa gorge at the city's

---

[135] The same AC-130 gunships that had been denied to Task Force Ranger in 1993.

entrance, but by that afternoon, Northern Alliance forces overran the city from the south and west with the Taliban fleeing. The next day, Northern Alliance forces rounded up suspected Taliban fighters remaining in the city and executed them. Also on November 10, Northern Alliance forces took control of five northern provinces – the fall of Mazar-e-Sharif was the turning point of the war. Tribal commanders supporting the Taliban in the north quickly switched sides.

Taliban forces fled the capital city of Kabul in the face of advancing Northern Alliance forces on the night of November 12. It took approximately 15 minutes to deal with a dozen or so remaining Taliban fighters. With the fall of Kabul, the Taliban regime collapsed across the country over the next four days. By November 16, the residue of the Taliban was concentrated around their traditional stronghold of Kandahar while a group of mostly Pakistani Taliban fighters went to Konduz. By November 25, Taliban in Konduz surrendered. Most of the Konduz Taliban fighters were taken to a prison near Mazar-I-Sharif where an armed revolt of about 600 prisoners occurred. One casualty of the revolt was an American CIA employee, Mike Spann. It took Northern Alliance forces, supported by US aircraft, three days to put down the revolt. About 50 Northern Alliance soldiers were killed in the fighting. Less than 100 Taliban fighters survived. The incident was later characterized as a massacre by opponents of the war. In the aftermath of the prison uprising, an American Taliban fighter named John Walker was found among the surviving prisoners. His role in the uprising was unclear.

In Kandahar, Mullah Mohammed Omar, the Taliban leader began attempts to negotiate with Afghani tribal forces closing in on him from the east (shutting down his supply lines) on December 6. His plummeting morale was made worse by the arrival of US Marines on November 25. Omar wanted amnesty, but when the US Government rejected that proposal, he slipped out of the city. He was last seen on December 7 leaving town in a convoy of motorcycles literally headed for the hills. Other former Taliban leaders were able to escape to Pakistan. December 6 marked the end of any organized Taliban control anywhere in Afghanistan.

While the Taliban regime was imploding, Al Qaeda concentrated themselves in an extensive cave complex known as Tora Bora, about 30 miles southeast of Jalalabad. US Special Forces, along with local tribal fighters, were organized to attack while airstrikes pounded al Qaeda positions. Off and on fighting ended on December 17, 2001 when the last cave complex was captured. Bin Laden and other senior al Qaeda leaders were able to avoid capture, although a search of the caves continued until January.

In March, 2002, a buildup of al Qaeda and former Taliban was detected in the mountains of Shahi-Kot near Gardez. US forces launched "Operation Anaconda" to deal with what US intelligence believed was a small number of left-over fighters. The number of terrorist forces, much larger than anticipated – perhaps as high as 5,000 – effectively used hit and run tactics. No Americans had been lost while clearing Tora Bora, but eight were killed during "Anaconda". Over 400 Taliban and al Qaeda were reported killed, but only 50 bodies were found. Large numbers of terrorists escaped east into Pakistan, despite the fact that Pakistani forces were supposed to block escape routes.

In June 2002, the *Loya Jirga* (or "great council") met and appointed Hamid Karzai, a supporter of the former king of Afghanistan as interim president. Karzai, who had originally backed the Taliban, turned against them because of their close association with Pakistan. Following the Taliban's assassination of Karzai's father in 1999, he actively sought to overthrow the Taliban government. In January 2004, Afghanistan adopted a new constitution and held presidential elections in October and November. Karzai was elected president with 55% of the vote.

# *Iraq*

During his January 2002 State of the Union address, President Bush defined what he termed an "axis of evil", which included North Korea, Iran and Iraq. Describing each of these countries, he characterized them as capable of arming terrorists with weapons of mass destruction and called on nations to unite and "eliminate parasites who threaten their countries and our own."

Saddam Hussein's long history of invasion, use of chemical weapons against Iran and his own people, and non-cooperation with the United Nations weapons inspectors have already been documented. After "Desert Storm", Saddam attempted to assassinate former President George H. W. Bush during a visit to Kuwait in April 1993. Iraqi air defenses consistently fired at coalition (primarily British and American) aircraft enforcing the no fly zones in northern and southern Iraq. Saddam also took advantage of the "Oil for Food" program, designed to provide food and relief items to Iraqi citizens to mitigate the affects of the international embargo on Iraq. What Saddam was able to do was direct contracts and oil vouchers (vouchers to buy oil at discounted prices, and then sell for a profit on the market) in any way that he wished, apparently including providing vouchers to the program's UN director, Benon Sevan. According to documents recovered from Iraqi's Oil Ministry after the war, French, Russian and Chinese companies were also major beneficiaries. Saddam may also have channeled funds to a trust in Liechtenstein that the UN identified as being affiliated with al Qaeda, and a Swiss subsidiary of a Saudi firm that was close to the Taliban while bin Laden was in Afghanistan.[136] Saddam was also able to funnel "Oil for Food" funds to the families of

---

[136] Marc Perleman, "Oil for Food Sales Seen as Iraq Tie to Al Qaeda", *Forward*, http://www.forward.com/issues/2003/03.06.20/news2.html, June 20, 2003. Accessed August 23, 2005

Palestinian suicide bombers who attacked Israelis (thus subsidizing terrorists with US taxpayer funds).[137]

"Oil for Food" was not widely seen as an issue before the war, but spreading around money to key individuals and companies may have been a consideration for Russia, France and China, all members of the UN Security Council in opposing the war in 2003.

President Bush outlined his reasons for going to war with Iraq at an Allied conference on Iraq in the Azores in March 2003 in his "Moment of Truth" speech. At a press conference with the British Prime Minister, the Spanish President and the Prime Minister of Portugal, Bush said,

> The dictator of Iraq and his weapons of mass destruction are a threat to the security of free nations. He is a danger to his neighbors. He's a sponsor of terrorism. He's an obstacle to progress in the Middle East. For decades he has been the cruel, cruel oppressor of the Iraqi people.[138]

In short, the President's arguments were that Saddam had a history of using weapons of mass destruction (in fact in the next paragraph, he reminded the listeners that he used them on Iraqi citizens), that he was a serial aggressor, that he sponsored (and had ties to) terrorism, that he was an obstacle to peace in the Middle East, and that he was bad for the people of Iraq.

As in 1998, the issue of weapons inspectors and Iraq's reluctance to cooperate initiated a cycle that led to confrontation. However, there were two distinctions that led to different outcomes between 1998 and 2003: (1) the degree to which each

---

[137] "Probe: Oil-for-Food Money Went to Palestinian Bombers' Families", *Fox News* http://www.foxnews.com/story/0,2933,138759,00.html, November 17, 2004. Accessed September 27, 2005.

[138] George W. Bush, "Monday 'Moment of Truth' for World on Iraq", http://www.whitehouse.gov/news/releases/2003/03/20030316-3.html. Accessed August 23, 2005.

Administration was willing to go in dealing with Saddam and (2) 9-11. When President Clinton went to the Pentagon on February 17, 1998 to talk about Operation "Desert Thunder" and Iraq, he described "reckless acts of outlaw nations and an unholy axis of terrorists, drug traffickers and organized international criminals." Warning about this unholy axis, he said they,

> . . .will be all the more lethal if we allow them to build arsenals of nuclear, chemical and biological weapons and missiles to deliver them. We simply cannot allow that to happen. There is no clearer example of this threat than Saddam Hussein's Iraq. His regime threatens the safety of his people, the stability of his region and the security of all of the rest of us.[139]

President Clinton's statement is remarkably similar to President Bush's description of Iraq in his Azores press conference in March 2003. 9-11 did change everything. Three Administrations (Bush-Clinton-Bush) had allowed Saddam's regime to fester, with only pinprick reactions to his provocations. 9-11 put the world, and in particular nations that harbored terrorists, in a different light.

Near the end of the 1998 US-Iraq crisis, the Clinton Administration openly advocated a policy of regime change in Iraq. On October 31, 1998, Congress passed the "Iraq Liberation Act" (P.L. 105-338), making regime change in Iraq the law of the land in the United States.[140] In 2003, George Bush would finish what Bill Clinton started and implement federal law by removing Saddam from power.

During the summer of 2002, as events in Afghanistan were winding down (although bin Laden and Omar remained at large),

---

[139] Bill Clinton, "Text of Clinton Statement on Iraq" *CNN*, http://www.cnn.com/ALLPOLITICS/1998/02/17/transcripts/clinton. iraq/, Accessed August 23, 2005
[140] Kenneth Katzman, "Iraq: U.S. Efforts to Change the Regime", A Report to Congress (Order Code RL31339), updated October 3, 2002.

160

Saddam and the UN were in a showdown over UN weapons inspections. In August, US intelligence uncovered the sale of a prohibited chemical used to make solid fuels for Scud type missile systems by China to Iraq. The sale involved a French company that brokered the movement of 20 tons of chemicals, shipped from China to Syria, then moved into Iraq by truck. China and France denied the report. In September, President Bush went to the United Nations to request that they do something about Iraq or stand aside for a US led action. The Security Council responded in November by passing another in a series of resolutions (Resolution 1441) calling for the immediate and complete disarmament of Iraq. In October, Congress passed a Joint Resolution authorizing the use of force against Iraq. Meanwhile, in December, Iraq filed a weapons declaration report with the UN (in response to the November resolution) that weapons inspectors said was incomplete and was just repackaged information they had provided in 1997.

In January 2003, US intelligence reported that France had been selling prohibited spare part to Iraq for jet fighters and helicopters. Also in January, leaders of Britain, Spain, Italy, Portugal, Hungary, Poland, Denmark and the Czech Republic announced support for the United States in various newspapers. Meanwhile, a group of "human shield" volunteers assembled in London and departed for Iraq. Their presence was exploited by Saddam over the next couple of months, but most left in March, fearing that Saddam would, in fact, actually use them as human shields.

On February 5, 2003, Secretary of State Powell visited the UN and presented extensive data on Iraqi WMD production, evasion of UN weapons inspection attempts and links with al Qaeda. In the aftermath of this presentation, Hans Blix, the chief UN weapons inspector indicated that Iraq was making new efforts to cooperate. Within NATO, France, Belgium and Germany began to take a stand against cooperating in a war with Iraq. Austria restricted the use of their airspace for aircraft transiting in support of a war. In Iraq, inspectors discovered that

161

Iraqi al-Samoud 2 missiles had a range of 180 kilometers, exceeding the 150 kilometer restriction. Nevertheless, UN officials were unable to agree if the missile violated UN Security Council Resolution 1441. The fault lines that developed between the United States and larger nations of Western Europe were curious to many Americans. European dissent revolved in large part, around the inner circle of the European Union – France, Germany and Luxembourg. Newly liberated nations of Eastern Europe, along with Spain and Italy, and of course, Great Britain, gave strong support to the US. France's opposition can, perhaps, be attributed, to commercial (and "Oil for Food") interests in Iraq; determination to make the European Union an international counter to the United States; and, as some Bush Administration personnel claimed, France's determination to cling to past status as a great nation. Rumsfeld characterized this attitude as "Old Europe". Germany, a once staunch ally of the United States, had a basic pacifistic strain that emerged after the Cold War, according to military historian John Keegan. Keegan asserts that this "softer way" of the Germans became evident during the debate on Iraq.[141]

On February 14, Blix reported that Iraq was cooperating, but still had not accounted for all weapons known to exist or answered questions raised by Secretary Powell's presentation at the UN. On February 18, Turkey announced that it would not allow US ships to dock and unload troops and equipment unless the US increased a foreign aid grant from $6 billion to $10 billion. Many in the Bush Administration considered this blackmail. The situation with Turkey was complicated by the Kurdish desire to carve out an independent state in northern Iraq, and perhaps, southeastern Turkey. US support for the Kurds over the decade prior to the war in Iraq made many in the Turkish government wary of promises the US might offer the Kurds in return for their support against Saddam. The Turkish

---

[141] John Keegan, *The Iraq War* (New York: Alfred A. Knopf, 2004), 101.

demand was refused, and troops scheduled to transit Turkey were eventually rerouted to Kuwait.

On February 25, Britain, Spain and the US presented a draft resolution (follow-on to the November 2002 resolution) demanding Iraqi disarmament. France, Germany and Russia countered the resolution calling for peaceful disarmament through inspections. The next day, Blix reported that Iraq had not made a "fundamental decision" to disarm and that they refused to destroy the al-Samoud missiles. He also reported that one bomb discovered by inspectors could contain biological agents. And in Baghdad, newsman Dan Rather interviewed Saddam, who ruled out the possibility of exile to resolve the crisis.

On March 1, Iraq reversed itself and began destroying missiles while Turkey's Parliament voted to not allow US troops in Turkey. When Iraq started destroying missiles (while continuing to protest), the tone of UN inspection reports began to change, characterizing the Iraqis as more willing to cooperate. In early March, Bahrain, Kuwait and the United Arab Emirates called on Hussein to resign. By mid-March, Saddam opened training camps in Iraq for foreign fighters. Also in early March, US and British claims that Iraq had been attempting to buy "yellowcake" uranium were declared a fraud by Mohamed el Baradei, head of the International Atomic Energy Agency (see "Myths of the Iraqi War" at Appendix B for a discussion of the yellowcake issue).

On March 16, leaders of Britain, Portugal, Spain and the US met in the Azores. President Bush gave his "Moment of Truth" speech at a press conference on March 17. On the same day, the US advised UN weapons inspectors to leave Iraq and began removing non-essential personnel from Kuwait, Syria and Israel. Saddam turned down Bush's demand that he leave the country within 48 hours to avoid war. On March 19, US warplanes began bombing Iraqi artillery positions.

During "Desert Storm", the coalition ground forces facing Saddam's Iraq included two complete US Army corps (troop and equipment numbers can be found in Chapter Five), plus significant US Marine, British, French and Arab forces. During the 2003 invasion, dubbed operation "Iraqi Freedom", US and British ground forces were much smaller but even more lethal. On the Iraqi side, total regular army divisions had shrunk to seventeen and six Republican Guard Divisions. A new security force of three brigades that provided close protection for Saddam was named the Special Republican Guard. Most of the Iraqi equipment was poorly maintained due to shortage of parts and repair equipment because the international embargo interrupted the flow from most external suppliers. Another force (a surprise to most soldiers) that the new coalition faced was the *fedayeen* (martyrs), militia-like fighters who would prove to be the most deadly of all Iraqi forces. Members of the *fedayeen* included Ba'ath party members, some members of left-over militias established in the 1970's and, most notably, foreign fighters.

Norman Schwarzkopf's mantle as Combatant Commander, US Central Command fell to an extremely capable officer, General Tommy Franks. Franks found himself in a two front war – responsible for ongoing operations in Afghanistan and the new war in Iraq – so he delegated operations in Iraq to US Third Army Commander, Lieutenant General David McKiernan. Franks, who was the Third Army Commander during "Desert Thunder" in 1998, was very familiar with the Iraqi theater and had thought through combat operations in Iraq on several occasions. McKiernan's force included the US V Corps composed of bits and pieces of various divisions, including: 3$^{rd}$ Infantry Division; parts of the 101$^{st}$ Airborne Division (Air Assault) and 4$^{th}$ Infantry Division; a brigade of the 82$^{nd}$ Airborne Division; and later, the 173$^{rd}$ Airborne Brigade. McKiernan also had the 1$^{st}$ Marine Expeditionary Force (I MEF) which included the 1$^{st}$ Marine Division and Task Force Tarawa (which included a US Marine brigade and 3$^{rd}$ Marine Aircraft Wing). The UK provided the 1$^{st}$ Armored Division composed of the 7$^{th}$ Armored Brigade, the 16$^{th}$ Air Assault Brigade and 3$^{rd}$ Commando

Brigade (Royal Marines). 3$^{rd}$ Commando was attached to I MEF.

The coalition planned to invade Iraq from two directions – from the north, through Turkey, and from the south, through Kuwait. Turkey, first demanding more money, and then withdrawing permission to use their facilities, became a strategic and tactical problem. This left only one ground route into Iraq, a very narrow front from the south. Another option to introduce forces to northern Iraq, subsequently planned and used, was an airborne insertion.

Frank's basic plan was to send V Corps with their primary ground force, the 3$^{rd}$ Infantry Division to Baghdad on the south side of the Euphrates River while I MEF proceeded along the north side of the river. 1$^{st}$ UK Armored Division would drive north to seize Basra, while 3$^{rd}$ Commando with US support would take over the port of Umm Qasr and the Rumaila oil fields.

The air campaign, in contrast to weeks of bombing during "Desert Storm", would be short and precise and in conjunction with (not before) the ground campaign. The number of precision weapons available to the US Air Force in 2003 was comparatively large, and they were cheap. Global positioning system (GPS) guided gravity bombs resulted in a remarkably accurate weapon costing somewhere between $12,000 and $14,000 per strap on kit, compared to a Tomahawk Cruise Missile, which costs about $1.5 million apiece. Precision weapons could strike individual targets with less collateral damage than during "Desert Storm", and with a greater probability of success. During the first Gulf War, Iraqi military units were concentrated, making them more susceptible to large scale bombing. By 2003, Iraqi units were more scattered, thus harder to hit with non-precision weapons. Franks wished to minimize collateral damage and conduct a short campaign to reduce the amount of time available for Saddam to drum up support from neighboring Arab nations.

Success with the Northern Alliance in Afghanistan was largely due to Special Forces cooperation with and support of Northern Alliance units. Special Forces would have an important role in Iraq as well. Franks gave 48 US, UK and Australian Special Forces teams the responsibility to take care of key bridges across rivers and other classified tasks. Task Force 20, with elements of the 75th Ranger Regiment, operated in the western desert to cut routes from Iraq to Syria and take control of potential Scud missile launching sites.

D-Day was March 20, 2003, one day earlier than planned because of unscheduled airstrikes on Baghdad conducted in a failed attempt to kill Saddam and others. The Ramaila oil fields were quickly seized with little damage or opposition. The main ground attack began on March 22. Elements of I MEF were to seize a bridge in Nasiriyah for use by 3rd Infantry Division and I MEF as they streamed north. As Marines closed on Nasiriyah, *fedayeen* came by cars, motorcycles, and taxis – using any transportation available – to take them on. The battle that followed was "seized on gleefully by anti-American elements in the Western media to demonstrate that the war was not going the coalition's way."[142] Problems with trying to cram two large units through one small place with *fedayeen* attacking soon became apparent. Army and Marine units got mixed in the confusion, and the Army's 507th Maintenance Company became lost and separated, and was taken under fire. Nine soldiers were killed and six captured, including Jessica Lynch – the subject of the first successful prisoner of war (POW) rescue attempt in decades.

The 1st Battalion, 2nd Marines had been assigned to seize key bridge crossings (and were diverted to find and rescue remaining elements of the 507th). Although A Company was able to quickly seize the first bridge, C Company got involved in a firefight with *fedayeen* further along. With one vehicle on fire

---

[142] Keegan, 149.

166

and company leaders trying to organize resistance, a US Air Force A-10[143] fired at Marine vehicles and further wounded an already wounded Marine.

Fighting in Nasiriyah continued until the end of March, tying down Task Force Tarawa. Keegan points out that US Army reserve units had bridging equipment[144] in theater that could have been used to bypass Nasiriyah, thus denying *fedayeen* the opportunity to inflict casualties, slow down the advance and provide media coverage.

While the fight in Nasiriyah continued, I MEF and 3rd Infantry Division drove north – directly into a *shamal*, a dust storm which slowed movement and blew talcum powder quality dust into everything. At various times, rain and sleet mixed with dust and sand, making it difficult for troops to cope and keep equipment operating. By March 26, Major General Buford Blount III, commander of the 3rd Infantry Division, was having logistical difficulties. A "heavy" division, their combat power was in M-1 Abrams tanks, Bradley Fighting Vehicles, self propelled artillery and related supply intensive systems. They outran their capability to bring up supplies fast enough to keep them moving. Blount decided he needed to pause for resupply, and coordinated the halt with I MEF, V Corps and Third Army on March 27. The press immediately picked up on the pause, suggesting that the 3rd Infantry Division could be sitting on the road as long as 18-21 days.[145] The French press, in particular, was ecstatic over this development, gleefully predicting heavy American casualties.[146]

---

[143] A-10 Thunderbolt II (affectionately known as the "Warthog" because of its ugliness) is a single seat, twin engine jet aircraft designed specifically to support ground units. The aircraft is heavily armed with a 30 millimeter gatling gun and can carry Maverick and Sidewinder missiles.
[144] Keegan, 152.
[145] Ibid., 156.
[146] Ibid., 183.

Brigades of the 82$^{nd}$ Airborne Division and 101$^{st}$ Airborne (Air Assault) Division cleared for, and protected, the 3$^{rd}$ Infantry Division's left flank during the drive north. The 2$^{nd}$ Brigade, 82$^{nd}$ Airborne took Samawah in house to house fighting by April 4 and the 101$^{st}$ secured Najaf by April 1 and Hillah on April 10. (See Figure 4) The fight in Hillah was the only real organized resistance provided by regular Iraqi forces. In the north, the 173$^{rd}$ Airborne Brigade (from Italy) parachuted in to seize the airfield at Bashur and link up with *peshmerga* (Kurdish fighters) and Special Forces.

In the south, elements of 1$^{st}$ UK Armored Division began to invest Basra. Special Air Service (SAS) and Special Boat Service (SBS) teams, along with snipers, infiltrated the city while the division commander, Major General Robin Brims established a perimeter a distance away from the edge of the city. Brims' units watched and waited, and began collecting intelligence from the flow of refugees who learned that the British had food and water. Keegan reports that one reason Brims waited was to ensure minimal loss of life as he was under the hostile glare of the *BBC*, who took a decidedly anti-war stance in their coverage.[147]

Ali Hassan al-Majid, (a.k.a., "Chemical Ali") had responsibility for Basra's Iraqi defenses. Intensely hated by the locals and deserted by Iraqi Army units, Ali had to rely on barely trained *fedayeen*. He had little knowledge of British dispositions or capabilities, but he had one tool at his disposal – terror, and the population's knowledge of his willingness to use it.

Beginning on March 31, Brims began a large scale infiltration of the city by his units. Intelligence gleaned from SAS, SBS, snipers and refugees provided a clear picture of *fedayeen* locations and what Ali was doing. Snipers took an immediate and effective toll on Ba'ath party member moral with their long-range shots. They were able to immobilize the enemy

---

[147] Ibid, 177.

with no effect on the civilian population. Brims began what the Americans called "thunder runs", armed raids into the city, destroying previously identified targets, and then withdrawing. After several days of raids, Brims assaulted the city on April 6 and by April 8 was able to withdraw armored units and normalize the city by using walking patrols with soldiers in soft caps (no helmets) and carrying small arms. Years of experience in dealing with urban situations in Northern Ireland were expertly applied to Basra by Brims and his division.

The 3$^{rd}$ Infantry Division resumed their drive on March 30, after a brief (despite press predictions) logistics pause, heading for the Karbala Gap (a gap between Lake Razzazah on the west and the Euphrates River on the east). Using 82$^{nd}$ and 101$^{st}$ units to capture subsidiary objectives, Blount intended to draw out and engage the Republican Guard units outside of Baghdad and prevent them from retreating into the city. Blount's actions in the Gap were also intended to draw attention away from I MEF who was approaching the city from the southeast. To aid in the assault on the Gap, Rangers seized and held a key dam. 3$^{rd}$ Infantry tanks seized bridges and crossed the Euphrates on April 2 and drove toward the international airport. American presence at the airport resulted in attention from the *fedayeen*. Initial *fedayeen* efforts were unsupported by tanks or artillery and resulted in about 400 dead. A subsequent *fedayeen* attack included tanks, probably driven by Republican Guards. 3$^{rd}$ Infantry Division Abrams tanks destroyed approximately sixteen T-72 Iraqi tanks (their best equipment), and Bradley Fighting Vehicles destroyed five. By the next day, 3$^{rd}$ Infantry Division was in firm control of the airport complex, defeating an attempted Iraqi counterattack by destroying fourteen more Iraqi tanks. By 6 April, 3$^{rd}$ Brigade, 3$^{rd}$ Infantry Division was able to close Route 1 to the north of Baghdad, thus sealing main escape routes from the capital.

McKiernan and Franks agreed with Blount to launch "thunder runs" into Baghdad, similar to what Brims had done at Basra, but they did so without first infiltrating Special Forces units or snipers. The first run started early morning on April 5, 2003. The 1$^{st}$ Battalion, 64$^{th}$ Armor, supported by A-10s and attack helicopters, drove into an area of government ministries and palaces in the southern part of Baghdad. The Americans lost one M-1 Abrams tank to an RPG, but hundreds of *fedayeen* and Iraqi soldiers were killed in the raid, and several captured. Colonel Dave Perkins, commander of 3$^{rd}$ Infantry Division's 2$^{nd}$ Brigade checked *BBC* about how his run played with the international media, and found out that *BBC* reporters in Baghdad said they saw no evidence of American troops in the capital and concluded that such reports were false. The *BBC* report seemed designed to confirm the Iraqi Information Minister Muhammad Saeed al Sahhaf's (a.k.a., "Baghdad Bob" or "Comical Ali") claim that the Americans were being slaughtered at the airport and that none had entered Baghdad.[148] Hearing Sahhaf's report and *BBC's* tacit endorsement, Perkins decided that on the next run, he needed to take up permanent residence in Baghdad.

The next afternoon, Perkins briefed his commanders on the run set for April 7. He told them that the best way to get the word out that the Iraqi regime was doomed was to put M-1 Abrams Tanks and Bradley Fighting Vehicles into the middle of their objective palace complex overnight. That would demonstrate that the 3$^{rd}$ Infantry Division had control of the city – not Saddam – and would serve to counter effective Iraqi propaganda.

The 2$^{nd}$ Brigade, 3$^{rd}$ Infantry Division launched their April 7 run from the airport up Highway 8 into central Baghdad, establishing strongpoints at three overpasses they named "Larry", "Moe", and "Curly". The strongpoints were designed to receive and forward logistical vehicles needed to support the run and keep the route open. Sustained firefights developed around the strongpoints and *fedayeen* took a toll on resupply

---

[148] David Zucchino, *Thunder Run: The Armored Strike to Capture Baghdad*, (New York: Grove Press, 2004), 72.

vehicles. However, Perkins reached his objective, set up in the palace, fought off counterattacks and made American presence known. At the beginning of Perkins' run, a surface to surface missile struck his command post at the airport, killing five soldiers and damaging vehicles and equipment, but survivors quickly reorganized. During this and the previous run, troops faced *fedayeen* on foot, in taxi cabs, in "technical vehicles" (pickup trucks with a crew-served weapon of some type mounted – a term leftover from Somalia), and occasionally in an actual military vehicle. One of the most striking and distressing aspects of combat in Baghdad was the killing of Iraqi civilians in cars apparently on the way to work or to the market, going blissfully about their business because they believed Sahhaf's propaganda that the Americans were defeated and nowhere near Baghdad. Troops could not tell them from the many suicide car bombers hurtling against their positions and were forced to engage them, discovering in the aftermath the human wreckage, which unfortunately, included children.[149]

As Perkins moved to the city center, I MEF closed in from the southeast. On April 9, Marines arrived at Firdos Square and encountered one of countless Saddam statues. When they arrived, Iraqis were attempting to pull the statue down. With Marine help, the statue came down, an image that was seen around the world, giving lie to Sahhaf and causing distress among Saddam supporters. Keegan provides the perspective of a British military historian in recounting press reaction,

> As representatives of the *bien pensants* in Europe and even parts of North America, many television and print journalists declined to celebrate the fall of the dictator the toppling of his statue symbolized. Monster though he clearly was, his humiliation at the hands of the capitalist system – the United States, the world's largest economy, Britain, the fourth – rankled.[150]

---

[149] Keegan, 200.
[150] Ibid., 202.

The fall of the statue symbolically marked the end of organized combat. Saddam himself wasn't captured until December 13, 2003, when American troops found him hiding in a "spider hole" near his hometown of Tikrit. His two sons and a grandson were killed earlier in a shootout in Mosul in July 2003 with troops from the 101$^{st}$ Airborne Division and US Special Forces soldiers.

Cleanup continued after the end of "active combat", but for a time, most Americans assumed that the war was virtually over. They were wrong.

## *Opponents and the Anti-War Movement*

A quintessential example of the 2003 anti-Iraqi war movement in the United States was ANSWER, International (standing for "Act Now to Stop the War and end Racism"). ANSWER typified the anti-war movement that regenerated itself after 9-11. Formed as a coalition of several anti-war organizations on September 14, 2001, ANSWER became active the week after the 9-11 (the timing seems curious). The stated intent of the organization included challenging "war makers", building unity against racism, and defending civil rights and civil liberties.[151]   Just prior to the start of the invasion of Iraq, ANSWER claimed that they mobilized over 100,000 protestors in Washington DC, 100,000 in San Francisco and 50,000 in Los Angeles, and continued protests throughout the course of active combat. The Washington DC rally featured speeches from Jesse Jackson and US Congressman John Conyers, Jr. (D-MI), as well as performances from Willie Nelson and hip-hop artist Mos Def.

ANSWER's director was former Attorney General Ramsey Clark, who, at the same time, was working for Saddam Hussein as legal counsel to the Iraqi regime. Clark was also head of the

---

[151] ANSWER, http://www.internationalanswer.org/. Accessed August 25, 2005

172

International Action Center (IAC), which was founded by the Workers' World Party (WWP) in 1992 and was the direct parent organization of ANSWER. WWP is a Marxist based, communist party founded in the United States in 1959 and a strong supporter of remaining communist regimes including North Korea, Cuba and China. The WWP (and thus, ANSWER and IAC) expressed support for countries they considered to be the victims of "American Imperialism", such as Libya and Iraq. The non-theoretical nature WWP extended to anti-war protests against the invasion of Iraq in 2003 was typified by resurrected Vietnam era slogans instead of a rational basis for opposition.

ANSWER, IAP, WWP and supporting anti-war organizations were, and are, examples of radical cause-focused organizations. Representing the political leanings of its leader, ANSWER became an apologist for repressive regimes, regardless of ideology – from Iraq to North Korea. At the same time, a literature review of ANSWER coalition member organizations reveals an apparent attempt to ride an anti-war tide to gain support for their specific agendas, irrespective of the war. Though this paradigm may change over time, many related movements appear to be recasting themselves in the anti-Vietnam war mold, returning to the anti-American Cold War rhetoric ("imperialism', colonialism', "exploitive capitalism", etc.) recycled for the next generation.

Journalistic opposition to the invasion of Iraq has already been documented in Keegan's comments on the *BBC*, but additional examples provide a glimpse into American media opposition.

First, is Eason Jordan, a senior news executive at *CNN*. He disclosed on April 10, 2003 (the day after the statue of Saddam fell), that for years, *CNN* had repressed negative coverage of Saddam's brutality for fear of Iraqi retribution against members of *CNN*'s Baghdad bureau. The following day, Jordan wrote in an op-ed in the *New York Times* that

*CNN* did not report that an Iraqi cameraman who worked for *CNN* had been kidnapped, beaten and subjected to electric shocks; that Iraqi officials had attempted to kill *CNN*'s reporters in northern Iraq; and that "several Iraqi officials" had told him privately that Saddam "was a maniac who had to be removed." [152]

Jordan may have repressed Saddam's brutality against Western media for years, but he didn't have any qualms about making similar charges against American troops. In January 2005, Jordan stated at a World Economic Forum conference in Switzerland that coalition troops had "targeted" (killed) a dozen journalists in Iraq. Congressman Barney Frank (D-Mass), who was present during Jordan's remarks, later said that

Jordan seemed to be suggesting "it was official military policy to take out journalists." Jordan later "modified" his remarks to say that some US soldiers did this "maybe knowing they were killing journalists, out of anger," Frank said.[153]

Jordan's assertions that US troops were deliberately killing journalists were not initially reported by mainstream media representatives present at the conference, but were only made public because Internet "bloggers" published his comments. Jordan subsequently resigned.

Another example of biased media coverage was Peter Arnett, former *CNN* reporter who was stationed in Baghdad in 2003 for *National Geographic Television* and *NBC* News. Arnett gave an interview to Iraqi run state television on March 30, 2003 (in the midst of the 3rd Infantry Division pause for resupply) in which he said, "The first war plan has failed because of Iraqi resistance. Now they are trying to write another war plan. Clearly the

---

[152] "Grading TV's War News", Media Research Center, April 23, 2003, 9.

[153] Howard Kurtz, "CNN's Jordan Resigns Over Iraq Remarks", *Washington Post*, February 12, 2005.

American war planners misjudged the determination of the Iraqi forces."[154]   Arnett also praised the Iraqi regime for their openness to journalists during the course of the war – even though Iraq had expelled several journalists and imprisoned two reporters from *Newsday* during the time the interview was given. Arnett further said,

"President Bush says he is concerned about the Iraqi people, but if Iraqi people are dying in numbers, then American policy will be challenged very strongly," he said.  In their interview, Arnett said reports from Baghdad on civilians being killed are being shown in the United States, and "it helps those who oppose the war when you challenge the policy to develop their arguments."[155]

Arnett indicated that his reports from Baghdad during the war "would tell the Americans about the determination of the Iraqi forces, the determination of the government and the willingness to fight for their country".[156]  *NBC* issued a statement supporting Arnett after the interview was aired, but then fired him the next day.  *National Geographic* responded immediately by firing Arnett.

And what about other journalists' views on Arnett?   On March 31, Matt Lauer interviewed Arnett on the *Today Show*. Arnett insisted that American planners had failed and that his view was consistent with other media opinions.  Lauer then said to Arnett, "Peter, at the risk of getting myself in trouble, I want to say I respect the work you've done over the last several weeks and I respect the honesty with which you've handled this situation.  So good luck to you."  Lauer certainly did not get in trouble.   In the April 5 edition of *TV Guide* (comments presumably made before the Iraqi television interview), Arnett

---

[154] "Peter Arnett: US War Plan has Failed", March 31, 2003, http://www.cnn.com/2003/WORLD/meast/03/30/sprj.irq.arnett/. Accessed August 25, 2005
[155] Ibid.
[156] Ibid.

said "The Iraqis have let me stay because they see me as a fellow warrior. They know I might not agree with them, but I've got their respect."

The late Peter Jennings, *ABC* News anchor reflected on the toppling of Saddam's statue by Iraqis with Marine assistance. Jennings remarked, not on newly found Iraqi freedom, but strangely, on the plight of unemployed statue artists.

On April 9, the day US Marines helped Iraqi civilians topple a huge statue of Saddam, Jennings anchored *ABC*'s live coverage. As the statue collapsed to the sound of Iraqi cheers, the *ABC* anchor oddly remarked about the willingness of Saddam to pose so often – as if the dictator was making some sort of sacrifice – and wistfully reflected on how the sculptors who made such monuments to tyranny will have nothing to do now that freedom has arrived in Iraq: "Saddam Hussein may have been, or may be, a vain man, but he has allowed himself to be sculpted heavy and thin, overweight and in shape, in every imaginable costume – both national, in historic terms, in Iraqi historic terms – in contemporary, in every imaginable uniform, on every noble horse. The sculpting of Saddam Hussein, which has been a growth industry for 20 years, may well be a dying art."[157]

In apparent support of anti-war activism, Jennings complained to Senator Joe Biden (D-Del) on air on March 20 that the Democratic Party was abandoning their anti-war constituents. Then, on the night of March 21, during a one-hour program on the war, Jennings aired three taped pieces on anti-war protestors and dissenters. One piece, eight minutes long, was dedicated to two left-wing protestors. Jennings also remarked on low levels of college student participation (apparently in comparison to Vietnam) in the protest movement, "The college campus appears rather quiescent to some – quite."

---

[157] "Grading TV's War News", Media Research Center, April 23, 2003, 3.

On the other hand, *ABC*'s *World News Tonight* could not find time to cover a "support the troops" rally (15,000 participants) in New York City on April 10.[158]

Another example of basic media assumptions about the nature of the conflict, related to the 3$^{rd}$ Infantry Division's tactical pause, was an exchange between Leslie Stahl of *CBS* with Colin Powell on March 25, 2003.

> **Leslie Stahl**: "The Powell Doctrine in military terms is that you throw a massive force, if you're going to war, make it huge. There are now criticisms, we're beginning to hear, that this force isn't massive enough."
> **Colin Powell**: "It's nonsense . . . The United States armed forces, with our coalition partners – the British principally, and the Australians – have gone 300 miles deep into Iraq in a period of five days. That is a heck of an achievement."
> **Stahl**: "Yeah, but our, the rear is exposed."
> **Powell**: "It's not. Exposed to what?"
> **Stahl**: "Exposed to Fedayeen, exposed . ."
> **Powell**: "Fine. So? We'll get them in due course . ."
> **Stahl**: Are you saying you're not worried or concerned about guerilla warfare?"
> **Powell**: "Of course we are and that, and we're trained to handle this . . They're not threatening the advance."
> **Stahl**: "But you can't get your supplies, you can't . ."
> **Powell**: "Who says?"
> **Stahl**: ". . can't get the humanitarian . ."
> **Powell**: "Who says?"
> **Stahl**: ". . can't get the humanitarian aid in there."
> **Powell**: "Only because the minefields haven't been cleared at the port of Umm Qasr . . The situation will change rapidly."[159]

---

[158] Ibid., 4.
[159] Ibid., 6.

During "Desert Storm", US military leaders attempted to control the press by establishing reporter pools and trying to keep the press away from the troops and combat. That approach, designed to avoid the type of coverage experienced during Vietnam, drew heavy criticism from across the media spectrum. In 2003, "embedded" reporters were allowed to operate with specific units during the course of the war. The "embed" approach allowed immediate combat coverage and relatively unfettered access (as long information did not reveal details of current or future operations). In addition to providing live combat coverage, two things became apparent. First, embedded reporters naturally developed a close relationship with the units to which they were assigned. Combat comradeship created sympathetic coverage. Second, embedded reporters, away from the political orientation of their bosses, often found themselves at odds with the network anchors and editors in New York or London. This created some interesting tensions, particularly at *BBC*.

General political opposition to the war came from liberal Democrats. Two, in particular, made themselves known during the course of the Iraqi invasion – Congressman John Conyers and former Governor and Democratic Presidential Candidate Howard Dean (D-VT). In March 2003, even before the invasion began, Conyers, along with former Attorney General and ANSWER director Ramsey Clark, convened a meeting in Washington DC to finalize articles of impeachment against President Bush for "high crimes and misdemeanors" for planning preemptive action against Iraq. Later, after the war started, Conyers spoke at ANSWER organized anti-war rallies. He spoke in opposition to preemptive action, but Conyers' general objections to the war (at that time) were vague, and basically revolved around inappropriate expenditures of funds, that could be used, instead, to help the poor.

Howard Dean's anti-war approach was different. His opposition was not to the use of combat power, but to the President's unilateral application of power in Iraq. Unlike

Conyers, Clark and ANSWER, Dean outlined his opposition logically,

> One, unilateral action is not appropriate unless there is an imminent threat to the United States. Two, the imminent threat would consist of Iraq's having a nuclear program or developing one or being found, credibly, giving weapons of mass destruction, such as chemical or biological weapons, to terrorists. Three, Saddam needs to be disarmed, period, whether he's an imminent threat or not. Four, the responsibility for disarming Iraq belongs right now to the UN because Saddam is an imminent threat to the region . . . Unilateral action is not appropriate.[160]

## *Conclusion*

Both the invasion of Afghanistan and of Iraq were unequaled military successes. They were fast, imaginative and resulted in limited coalition and civilian casualties – and both were accomplished with much smaller combat forces than could have been envisioned only ten years before. With a head start, a constitution and an elected government in Afghanistan, along with a general perception of security, the Afghan democratic experiment moved ahead of efforts in Iraq. Post-invasion Iraq proved difficult – with many mistakes made by the interim provisional authority aided and abetted by foreign fighters, hardcore Ba'athists, criticism in the US, the unacceptable behavior of prison guards at Abu Ghraib and a neglectful chain of command.

Troubles in helping post-war Iraq to recover quickly drew critics, temporarily muted by the military victory. Bush was accused of focusing on Iraq while ignoring the real source of terror – al Qaeda. However,

---

[160] David Corn, "Howard Dean", *The Nation*, March 31, 2003.

"Critics have assailed President Bush for his strategy on terrorism, calling the war in Iraq a diversion from the main task of defeating al Qaeda. But just days after the 60th anniversary of victory in World War II, it is striking to note how Franklin D. Roosevelt faced very similar critics and how President Bush has adopted a grand strategy very much in the Roosevelt tradition," Peter Schweizer writes in *USA Today*.

"With a logic that Bush would find familiar, FDR was lambasted by his critics for his WWII military strategy of defeating Germany first before focusing on Japan. They consider Germany a diversion. Wasn't it Japan and not Germany that had attacked us at Pearl Harbor, asked Sens. Arthur Vandenberg and A. B. Chandler? One foreign minister called the idea 'suicidal heresy'.

"By 1942, American generals were complaining that precious resources were being diverted to fight Germans in North Africa, hardly a direct strategic concern. All of this should sound familiar in the debate over Iraq and the war on terrorism," said Mr. Schwiezer, a research fellow at the Hoover Institution.[161]

But of course, the "War on Terror" did extend beyond Afghanistan and Iraq. Remarkable changes began in the Middle East, including the Libyan renunciation of WMD and a tentative move toward democratic based nations in the region – notably Lebanon. As encouraging as these developments are, however, the Middle East is far from becoming a thoroughly democratized region. Islamic fundamentalism and old line regimes pull the spirit of freedom in different directions. Furthermore, the US has a legacy, going back to Vietnam, for not staying the course. Terrorists and terrorist supporting states learned to rely on that certainty, and likely do so today. A key difference is that the

---

[161] Greg Pierce, "Inside Politics", *The Washington Times*, August 18, 2005

North Vietnamese never threatened to invade the United States, to destroy our institutions or way of life – America's enemies in the "War on Terror" have done so, and have demonstrated that they will continue to work to achieve their objectives.

## Chapter Eight

# Conclusion – Now and Then

*"They (the North Vietnamese) were learning quickly that they need not win the offensive, but only overrun for a few days purportedly secure areas in order to cause a firestorm of recrimination and unrest in America."*

Victor Davis Hanson

The task of reconstructing history requires that the reconstructionist (a person rewriting or revising history) work from a basic philosophical framework. The prevailing view of those currently writing history (at least within standard college textbooks) is that the United States consistently gets it wrong, that Americans are inherently intent on stripping the world of resources and that Americans are hoarding democracy for ourselves. Bevin Alexander disagrees with this anti-American bias, and in his book, *How America Got it Right*, he describes the basic American view as generally wanting to do the right thing.

This inclination to do right has been virtually unique among the nations of the world, and for this reason we have been often misunderstood. How could a country so rich and successful be so unselfish and caring? We *must* have darker motives, critics say. We *must* be seeking to create an empire, to dominate everyone else, to grab the oil or the trade or whatever else for our own selfish purposes. People from more grasping, less-idealistic societies find it impossible to accept that we honestly believe that giving everyone opportunity is the recipe for abundance and happiness everywhere, not merely in the favored reaches of the United States of America. We honestly believe that securing other people's freedom is the best guarantee that we can keep our own.[162]

Describing history as it happened, and then drawing conclusions based on factual information was the objective of historians in past decades. Even so, historians' philosophies and agendas have always guided their assessments and conclusions (from Herodotus to the present), but generally not their retelling of the facts. Where some contemporary historians depart from the past is their wholesale mistreatment of factual information. Whether by failing to check facts, omitting factual information or deliberately falsifying data – some influential historians have been active participants in allowing myths and legends to enter mainstream history, and have become useful in supporting philosophical agendas.

So, how can history stay "unreconstructed"? History can only be reconstructed (revised) when historians, students, the media, universities and readers of history allow it to happen. Along these lines, I have some reconstruction prevention suggestions. First, beware the myth – popular legends designed to achieve an agenda or energize a political base. Myths of Iraq are "out there" and widely believed. They are reinforced by evening news, reporters and editorials. Readers only have to look as far as David Corn's opinion piece, cited in Appendix B, to see myths in the midst of creation. In the past, literary and textual critics spent lifetimes attempting to discover the origins of various myths. Today, we have the rare opportunity of watching the myth-making process unfold on the evening news. Fortunately, uncovering myths requires only a modicum of research for those willing to spend a few minutes checking the facts. Unfortunately, myths powerfully encapsulate and transmit "received truth" for many, and often go un-refuted by the mainstream press, who serve to transmit selected myths. An excellent example of mythmaking as an effective art supported

---

[162] Bevin Alexander, *How America Got it Right: The US March to Military and Political Supremacy*, (New York: Crown Forum, 2005), 3.

by mainstream media is *CBS'* Mark Knoeller's interview with anti-war activist, Cindy Sheehan. Knoeller asked Sheehan, "You know that the president says Iraq is the central front in the war on terrorism, don't you believe that?" Sheehan replied,

> No, because it's not true. You know Iraq was no threat to the United States of America. Iraq was not involved in 9-11, Iraq was not a terrorist state. But now that we have decimated the country, the borders are open, freedom fighters from other countries are going in, and they (American troops) have created more terrorism by going to an Islamic country, devastating the country and killing innocent people in that country. The terrorism is growing and people who never thought of being car bombers or suicide bombers are now doing it because they want the United States of America out of their country.[163]

This interview contains myths uncritically retransmitted by the mainstream press for broad consumption. Even assuming that Iraq was not directly involved in 9-11 (an unresolved question), the rest of Sheehan's statements are patently false, easily verified and can be refuted point by point. Her statements, in particular, regarding the wanton wholesale killing of innocent civilians by American troops appear to be tired repackaging of John Kerry's 1971 allegations before the United States Senate Foreign Relations Committee.

Second, beware of bent history – history that is rewritten or created to support preconceived political agendas, but masquerading as legitimate scholarly work. In 2000, Dr. Michael Bellesiles, a professor at Emory University, published a book entitled *Arming of America: Origins of a National Gun Culture* in which he attacked and attempted to disprove long held theories among historians that gun ownership was widespread in

---

[163] Joe Kovacs, "Cindy: Terrorists 'freedom fighters'", *World Net Daily*, August 23, 2005, http://www.worldnetdaily.com/news/article .asp?ARTICLE_ID 45938, Accessed August 24, 2005.

early America.  He based his conclusions on research using early American probate records.  His book was an instant hit and garnered him Columbia University's Bancroft Prize for the best work of American history published in 2000.  Over time, however, researchers began to take a closer look at Bellesiles' research and reported serious inconsistencies (misusing facts or creating evidence).  For example, Bellasiles contended that early Americans did not widely possess guns because they were expensive and inefficient, that people did not know how to use them, and that hunting was an unnecessary luxury.  Because his conclusions seemed to be so inconsistent with the facts among those familiar with probate research, Emory University appointed an investigating committee which concluded that Bellesiles was "guilty of both substandard research methodology and of willfully misrepresenting specific evidence in *Arming America.*"[164]  In fact, as Joyce Lee Malcolm reports in the March 2003 issue of the journal *Reason*, Bellesiles "repeatedly twists the truth to fit (his) thesis".  This type of reconstruction is harder to detect, and often requires specialists, dedicated to uncovering the truth by checking research methods and underlying data.  Fortunately, in the case of Bellesiles, his conclusions were novel enough to attract serious academic scrutiny.

Third, beware of factual emphasis – the heavy use of information to support a given agenda at the expense of a balanced view of history.  An example is the heavy emphasis William Perry placed on Mikhail Gorbachev's involvement in the demise of the Soviet Union, while virtually ignored Ronald Reagan's contributions, which are documented in Chapter Four.

Beyond the spinning or reconstructing of history, is the use of history itself.  For many, reading history is a pleasure that has no other end.  But history has much to teach us – as individuals and as a nation.  A consistent theme of this book is that

---

164 Michael de la Merced, "Bellesiles resigns as fraud investigation ends", The Emory Wheel online, www.emorywheel.com/vnews/disiplay.v/ART/2002/10/25/3db9bc0a08df2, Accessed August 30, 2005.

American's enemies have learned over the past 40 years that the United States does not stand fast, but retreats in the face of danger. Successive presidents reinforced that perception – from Nixon in Vietnam, to Carter in Iran, to Reagan in Lebanon, to Clinton in Somalia. At this writing, many in Congress and among the political elite are calling for America to withdraw from Iraq – they either do not see the historical trend, or do not care. My conclusion is that an early exit from Iraq would be another instance of failed American promises, in this case of promises made to Iraqi citizens and to Americans who seek a more secure environment to raise their families and ensure the continuation of liberty.

Throughout the history of our nation, there have been those who looked for a constructive solution. General Harold Johnson recognized American failures in Vietnam and crafted a strategy to make South Vietnam secure and "win" the war. Unfortunately, President Johnson and General Westmoreland ignored him until the nation turned against the war. Ronald Reagan knew that the Soviet Union was vulnerable and undertook a campaign to end the Soviet threat to American security. Jimmy Carter persevered in the face of universal pessimism and concluded a lasting peace agreement between Egypt and Israel. As a matter of history, when constructive approaches were pursued, our nation and the world became more secure. When we turned our backs on that which was hard and took the easy path, our nation paid ultimately paid a price.

We are all historians. Possessing a history degree doesn't mean that an individual has a corner on the market – only a good starting point and exposure to the process of writing and evaluating historical events. All of us live inside of history, are the products of the past, and expect that history will continue into the future. We experience history first-hand. We hold views about how factual some information may be (is it real, bent or mythical?) and draw conclusions based on our assessment of that information. How well we "do" history affects our view of reality: our view of God and salvation, how we vote, how we

186

plan for the future, what we read, and even our associations with other people.

My challenge to you, the reader, is to critically evaluate what you read, see, or hear. Never accept information (including what you read in this book) at face value – check it. Draw your own conclusions.

## Appendix A

# The Myths of Vietnam

*"No event in American history is more misunderstood than the Vietnam War. It was misreported then, and it is misremembered now. Rarely have so many people been so wrong about so much. Never have the consequences of their misunderstanding been so tragic."*

Richard Nixon

This summary of Vietnam War myths and truths was originally organized around a speech given by Lieutenant General James Link (US Army, Retired), former commander of Redstone Arsenal, AL, who delivered his address at a breakfast commemorating the arrival of the traveling Vietnam Veterans' Memorial Wall in Huntsville, AL. I used General Link's remarks as the starting point for an information paper, used in college history classes, to correct textbook errors. Over time, the focus and content of this paper has changed, but the basic outline remains, essentially, General Link's speech.

**First Myth**: US Armed Forces suffered a military defeat in Vietnam.

**Truth**: This myth has been repeated as fact in various publications, including college textbooks. For example, on page 1160 of Gillon and Matson's *The American Experiment*, the authors state that the "military failure in Vietnam, despite its enormous advantage in firepower, underscored the fundamental problem with America's Vietnam policy." In William Perry's *Western Civilization: A Brief History (Fourth Edition)*, he wrote, "The government shipped to Vietnam nearly half a million soldiers equipped with the most advanced chemical weapons and electronic equipment available. Yet victory eluded the American forces." Finally, Perry concludes with "In 1975, the North Vietnamese swept aside the inept South Vietnamese army and unified the country under a communist dictatorship. Ho Chi Minh had triumphed against the mightiest nation in the world." Actually, US forces were never defeated in battle, and the war was not lost on the battlefield. In fact, US forces defeated the enemy whenever they found them. After the North Vietnamese Tet Offensive in 1968, the Viet Cong and North Vietnamese operating in South Vietnam were so soundly defeated that they could not launch another major offensive until 1972. But the setback in 1968 did not deter the North Vietnamese; they were willing to lose the war on the battlefield because they were after victory in the minds of the American people.[165]

In 1968, Walter Cronkite interviewed General Fred Weyand. Cronkite acknowledged the American victory during the Tet battles, but told Weyand he preferred to report on the thousands of Vietnamese he had seen being put in mass graves in the ancient city of Hue after Tet. In reporting this, rather than any American victory, he said he hoped to bring a quicker end to the war. It didn't seem to bother Mr. Cronkite that the bodies were those of South Vietnamese brutally killed by the North Vietnamese during Tet. Nor did it seem to bother him that he had compromised his own objectivity and integrity in reporting the war. Mr. Cronkite implied that if America stopped fighting the war, that the Viet Cong and North Vietnamese would stop killing innocent civilians, thus making Americans responsible for those deaths.

**Second Myth:** Soldiers that served in Vietnam were largely minority and underprivileged youths.

**Truth.** This myth relates that somehow the soldiers in Vietnam were very different from those that served in World War II. The myth purports that the Vietnam soldier was much younger, poorly educated, and forced to go to war against his will (see

---

[165] From a speech by General William Westmoreland before the Third Annual Reunion of the Vietnam Helicopter Pilots' Association (VHPA) at Washington DC on July 5, 1986. General Westmoreland is quoting Douglas Pike, University of California, Berkley.

page 1161 of Gillon and Matson which says, "The majority of the young men who fought in Vietnam came from either poor or working class backgrounds. Many youths from middle-class families used a liberal student deferment policy to avoid the draft.") It is often claimed that soldiers who fought in Vietnam came mostly from minority groups, while their better-off social superiors dodged the draft and stayed safe at home, out of harm's way. The truth is, of course, different. The average age of all soldiers in Vietnam was nearly 24 years[166] (not the 19 years cited by Gillon and Matson on page 1161) compared to around 26[167] in World War II, where mass conscription prevailed. A related myth says that the average <u>infantry</u> soldier was 19 years old (see the text again). Assuming those killed in Vietnam accurately represent age groups serving, the average age of an infantry soldier was actually 22. None of the enlisted grades had an average age of less than 20.[168] The enlisted soldier in Vietnam was actually better educated than his World War II counterpart: 79%[169] of Vietnam War soldiers completed high school as opposed to just 24% for soldiers in World War II. In Vietnam, 20% of the enlisted men had college degrees, three times the number in World War II. The 19 year old claim is repeated throughout the histories of the era as indicated in this quote from the *Encarta* article on the Vietnam War.

> The escalating war, however, required more draftees. In 1965 about 20,000 men per month were inducted into the military, most into the Army, by 1968 about 40,000 young men were drafted each month to meet increased troop levels ordered for Vietnam. The conscript army was largely composed of teenagers; the average age of a US soldier was

---

[166] Information regarding the average age of soldiers during the Vietnam war from the Combat Area Casualty File (CAFC), November 1993, which is the comprehensive file of deaths used as the database for creation of the Vietnam Memorial in Washington DC, Center for Electronic Records, the National Archives.
[167] Westmoreland.
[168] CACF.
[169] Edward J. Marolda, *By Sea, Air and Land*

19. Those conscripted were mostly youths from the poorer section of American society, who did not have access to the exemptions that were available to their more privileged fellow citizens.[170]

The *Encarta* article appears to support contention with facts. The facts, however, are misapplied. As far as social representation among soldiers that actually served in Vietnam (as opposed to draftees in general), studies have shown that African-Americans and Hispanics were actually slightly underrepresented compared to their percentage of the total population. For instance, African-Americans comprised 12.5% of the age group subject to the military; they comprised 10.6% of those that served in Vietnam, and represented 12.1%[171] of the casualties in Vietnam (see page 1161 of the Matson and Gillon regarding discussion of African-Americans serving in Vietnam). In 1992, a study looked at the approximately 58,000 Americans killed in Vietnam and found that 30% came from families in the lowest third of the income range, while 26% came from the highest.[172] In fact, those from higher income levels tended to have a slightly more elevated risk of death because they were more likely to be pilots or infantry officers (also see the Third Myth below and the *Encarta* article).

**Third Myth**: Enlisted men were killed at a much higher rate than officers.

**Truth**: While officers killed in action accounted for 13.5% of those who died in Vietnam, they comprised only 12% of troop

---

[170] "Vietnam War", *Microsoft ® Encarta ® Encyclopedia*, 2001 © 1993-2000 Microsoft Corporation.
[171] Ray Smith, "Vietnam War Myths", utilizing CACF statistical data http://www.rjsmith.com/war_myth.html#service. Accessed October 21, 2005. and "Vietnam War Statistics", cited from *VFW Magazine*, January 1998, www.webmaganet./kman/nfv6.htm. Accessed October 22, 2005. Another good source is "Statistics about the War in Vietnam", http://www.vhfcn.org/stat.html. Accessed October 27, 2005.
[172] VFW generated figures (cited in the previous footnote) indicate that 50% of those served had middle class backgrounds.

strength. Proportionally, more officers were killed in Vietnam than in World War II. In Vietnam, the US lost twice as many company commanders as platoon leaders.

**Fourth Myth**: Draftees died at alarming rates in Vietnam.

**Truth**: Volunteers, not draftees, accounted for the majority (70%)[173] of combat deaths during the war. During Vietnam, something over 2,000,000 men were drafted. At the same time, 8,000,000 men volunteered for service in Vietnam. The volunteers who served and died there far outnumbered the draftees.

**Fifth Myth**: President Johnson made up the "Gulf of Tonkin Incident"

**Truth**: On page 1157 of Matson and Gillon, the authors indicate that the Gulf of Tonkin incident was fabricated. In fact, there were two incidents reported. The first was an attack by North Vietnamese patrol boats on the *USS Maddox* and *USS Turner Joy* on August 2, 1964 while American ships were involved in intelligence gathering efforts. The aircraft carrier *USS Ticonderoga* sent aircraft to repel the North Vietnamese attackers and sank one boat while damaging other enemy vessels. The second incident, the one referred to by Matson and Gillon which reportedly occurred on August 4, 1964, was either made up by the captain of the *USS Maddox*, or his crew misread their instruments and assumed that they were under attack. The

---

[173] From a speech by Lieutenant General Barry R. McCaffrey (reproduced in the Pentagram, June 4, 1993) assistant to the Chairman of the Joint Chiefs of Staff, to Vietnam veterans and visitors gathered at "The Wall", Memorial Day, 1993. At variance with McCaffrey's 70% statement is Ray Smith's claim that 62% of those killed were volunteers, http://www.rjsmith.com/war_myth.html#service. Accessed October 21, 2005. Both McCaffrey and Smith's numbers indicate that the overwhelming majority of those killed were not draftees.

vexing issue is that the authors chose to omit the real (first) attack from discussion in the text.[174]

**Sixth Myth**:  Americans indiscriminately killed large numbers of civilians.

**Truth**:  Matson and Gillon claim on page 1160 that "1.4 million civilians died or were wounded <u>by American forces</u>" (emphasis added).  The Pentagon and the US Senate estimates that the total killed and wounded by actions from all sides (North Vietnamese Army, Viet Cong, South Vietnamese Army and the US Armed Forces) at about the same[175] (apparently implying that all casualties during the war were generated by US forces).  There were twice as many casualties in the first two years after the fall of Saigon in 1975 than there were during all the years of US involvement in Vietnam.[176]  According to the government of Cambodia, a conservative estimate of those killed (not just wounded) in Cambodia by the communist *Khmer Rouge* regime under Pol Pot after the fall of Vietnam is approximately 1.7 million people, but Cambodians in exile put the number as high as 3 million.  During the war, the Viet Cong routinely executed civilians.  In Hue City during the 1968 Tet Offensive, an estimated 4,000 to 6,000 people were executed by the Viet Cong.[177]  The bottom line is that the text offers a number representing civilian casualties caused by US forces, without listing a source for that statistic, or any statistics that are at odds with the Pentagon, US Senate or even a statistic from the government of communist Vietnam.

---

[174]Thomas G. Patterson, J. Garry Clifford and Kenneth J. Hagen, *American Foreign Relations: A History since 1895* (4th Edition) (Lexington: Heath and Company, 1995), 410.

[175] Contrast the 1.4 million estimate in the text with the Pentagon's final estimate of total civilian casualties (killed and wounded by all sides) at 1,225,000 and a US Senate Subcommittee report at 1,350,000, including 415,000 killed for the same period.

[176] 1996 *Information Please Almanac*

[177] Hanson, 394.

193

# The Myths of Iraq

In a *CBS News* opinion piece entitled, "Bashing Joe Wilson", columnist David Corn reinforced myths of the Iraqi war for future revisionist historians by summarizing the results of a Senate Intelligence Committee report on intelligence failures leading up the war in Iraq. He said, "The Senate intelligence committee's report on prewar intelligence demonstrates that George W. Bush launched a war predicated on false assertions about weapons of mass destruction and misled the country when he claimed Saddam Hussein was in cahoots with al Qaeda."[178]

Corn's implication is that the Bush Administration deliberately lied to the American people to gain support for the war. Actually, the report faulted the intelligence community for misleading the Administration. The Senate Intelligence Committee report concluded that the intelligence community failed to properly assess available intelligence and overstated Iraqi WMD capability. The reader will see later in this appendix that the President is not the only one that believed intelligence reports on Iraqi WMD capabilities. In fact, the Senate Intelligence Report concluded that the intelligence community failed to "accurately or adequately explain to policymakers the uncertainties behind the judgments in the October 2002 National Intelligence Estimate."[179] Regarding contacts between Iraq and al Qaeda, the Senate report summarized Defense Intelligence Agency (DIA) and CIA estimates on that subject and concluded that most contacts revolved around chemical and biological technical training by Iraq to al Qaeda, and that those contacts

---

[178] David Corn, "Bashing Joe Wilson", *CBS News*, July 20, 2004, www.cbsnews.com/stories/2004/07/20/opinion/main630711.shtml. Accessed October 20, 2005.
[179] Senate Intelligence Committee, *Report on the US Intelligence Community's Prewar Intelligence Assessment on Iraq*, July 7, 2004, 16.

were those that were generally mutually beneficial. In short, the Committee was forced to admit, in muted tones, that numerous contacts did exist between Al Qaeda and Iraq.

**First Myth**. George Bush lied to the American people when he claimed that Saddam Hussein had weapons of mass destruction.

**Truth**. Iraq used chemical weapons during their war with Iran and against Kurds in northern Iraq in 1988 (killing an estimated 5,000 people). The fact that Iraq produced, maintained and used chemical weapons is an incontrovertible fact. The issue is whether there was credible evidence that Saddam maintained weapons of mass destruction in 2003. In reviewing the status of Iraqi WMD programs in September 2002, the DIA Estimate said:

> A substantial amount of Iraq's chemical warfare agents, precursors, munitions, and production equipment were destroyed between 1991 and 1998 as a result of Operation Desert Storm and UNSCOM (United Nations Special Commission) actions. Nevertheless, we believe Iraq retained production equipment, expertise, and chemical precursors and can reconstitute a chemical warfare program in the absence of an international inspection regime . . . There is no reliable information on whether Iraq is producing and stockpiling chemical weapons, or where Iraq had – or will – establish its chemical warfare agent production facilities . . . Iraq is steadily establishing a dual use industrial chemical infrastructure that provides some of the building blocks necessary for production of chemical agents.

The National Intelligence Estimate (NIE), published October 1, 2002, included the following statements about Iraqi WMD capabilities: that Iraq "is reconstituting its nuclear program"; "has chemical and biological weapons"; was developing unmanned aerial vehicles "probably intended to deliver biological warfare agents"; and that "all key aspects – R&D (research and development), production and weaponization – of Iraq's offensive BW (biological warfare) program are active and that most elements are larger and more advanced than they were before the Gulf War" [180] This NIE was a key document, used not only by the Administration to judge Iraqi WMD capabilities, but Congress, the UN and other intelligence services.

Based on the NIE, and other intelligence community documents, the United Nations, US intelligence agencies and other intelligence organizations all concluded that Hussein either had or could quickly produce weapons of mass destruction – chemical weapons in particular. Their view was shared by others – such as members of the US Congress.

> There is no doubt that . . . Saddam Hussein has invigorated his weapons programs. Reports indicate that biological, chemical and nuclear programs continue apace and may be back to pre-Gulf War status. In addition, Saddam continues to redefine delivery systems and is doubtless using the cover of a licit missile program to develop longer-range missiles that will threaten the United States and our allies. (Letter to President Bush signed by Senator Bob Graham [D-FL] and others, December 5, 2001)
>
> We know that he has stored secret supplies of biological and chemical weapons throughout his country (Al Gore, September 23, 2003, former Senator and Vice-President).
>
> Without question, we need to disarm Saddam Hussein. He is a brutal, murderous dictator, leading an oppressive regime . . . . He presents a particularly grievous threat because he is so consistently prone to miscalculation . . . And now he is miscalculating America's response to his continued deceit and his consistent grasp for weapons of mass destruction. So the threat of Saddam Hussein with weapons of mass destruction is real. (Senator John F. Kerry, [D-MA], January 23, 2003.

---

[180] Senate Intelligence Committee Report, 14.

The above quotes from members of Congress are most certainly based on the best intelligence that they had at the time they made each statement. President Bush relied on the same information.

WMD elements have been found in Iraq since the war. For example, the *BBC* reported that on June 23, 2004, the US removed 1.77 metric tons of enriched uranium from Iraq to prevent the material becoming available to third world nations or terrorists for production of nuclear weapons.[181] Chemical artillery, rocket and mortar rounds containing nerve and mustard agents have been found in Iraq. This includes chemical rounds used to make improvised explosive devices (IED). Terrorists even used mustard agents in a deliberate attack into the Green Zone in Baghdad.[182] Additionally, Polish soldiers were able to recover 17 rockets and 2 mortar shells sought by terrorists which contained nerve agents.[183]

Finally, regarding what may have happened to Iraqi WMD - a Syrian journalist indicated that Iraqi WMD had been moved to Syria and were located at three sites there, as of January 2004.[184]

President Bush did not deliberately fabricate intelligence or lie to the American people about WMD. He believed the same information that everyone else, from the United Nations to Congress, believed – Saddam Hussein had weapons of mass destruction.

---

[181] *BBC*, "US Reveals Iraq Nuclear Operation", http://news.bbc.co.uk/1/hi/world/middle_east/3872201.stm, July 7, 2004. Accessed October 21, 2005

[182] "1st Chemical Attack by Terrorists in Iraq", WorldNetDaily, June 26, 2005. www.worldnetdaily.com/news/article.asp?ARTICLE_ID=39158. Accessed October 21, 2005.

[183] Monika Scislowska, "Chermical Munitions Found by Polish Soldiers Were Being Pursued by Rebels", *C-News*, July 2, 2004.

[184] *WorldNetDaily*, "Syria Holding Iraqi WMD", www.worldnetdaily.com/news/article.asp?ARTICLE_ID=36463. Accessed October 21, 2005.

**Second Myth**.  President Bush lied in his 2003 State of the Union Address when he claimed that Iraq attempted to purchase "yellowcake" uranium from an African nation.

**Truth.** The Defense Intelligence Agency wrote a report on Iraqi attempts to obtain yellowcake uranium from Niger, a uranium producing nation in West Africa, in February 2002.  The paper was entitled, "Niamey Signed an Agreement to Sell 500 Tons of Uranium a Year to Baghdad" (National Military Joint Intelligence Center, Volume 028-02, February 12, 2002).  Vice President Cheney received a morning briefing on the report, and asked if the CIA agreed with the content.  In order to be able to answer the Vice President's question (since information in the DIA report came from the British), the CIA decided to investigate.  According to the Senate Intelligence Committee Report, CIA officials recalled that Ambassador Joseph Wilson was recommended by his wife, a CIA employee to go to Niger and determine whether or not the government there was contracting to sell yellowcake to Iraq.  Ambassador Wilson made the trip and met with the Nigerian official(s).  He did not prepare a report upon his return, but was debriefed at his home and indicated that Nigerian government officials were unaware of any contacts with Iraq regarding the sale of yellowcake.

In his 2003 State of the Union address, President Bush referred to intelligence reports about Iraqi attempts to buy yellowcake when he said, "The British government has learned that Saddam Hussein recently sought significant quantities of uranium from Africa."

In March 2003, Mohamed El Baradei, Director-General of the International Atomic Energy Agency (IAEA) told the UN Security Council that certain documents alleging Niger-Iraq yellowcake sales were forged, and that the IAEA had verified that fact.  Critics quickly jumped on these falsified documents, which various intelligence agencies later confirmed to be fabricated, to criticize the President and imply that American or

British intelligence had created documents for justification to go to war.

Ambassador Wilson wrote an op-ed piece in the *New York Times* (July 6, 2003), in which he accused the President of misusing intelligence regarding the Iraqi nuclear threat to justify the war. Wilson later admitted to the Senate Intelligence Committee staff that he was a source in a *Washington Post* article ("CIA Did Not Share Doubt on Iraq Data: Bush Used Report of Uranium Bid, *Washington Post*, June 12, 2003) in which claims were made that the yellowcake intelligence was based on the forged documents. The Senate Intelligence Committee staff, asking Wilson about the *Washington Post* article:

> . . . asked how the former ambassador could have come to the conclusion that the "dates were wrong and the names were wrong" (on the reports that El Baradei alleged were forged) when he had never seen the CIA reports and had no knowledge of what names and dates were in the reports. The former ambassador said that he may have "misspoken" to the reporter when he said he concluded the documents were "forged" (when he had never seen the documents and allegations of their forgery came out in March 2003, a year after Wilson was debriefed from his Niger trip on March 5, 2002).[185]

The contentious claim that Iraq and Niger had discussed purchase of yellowcake, despite Wilson's claims to the contrary and the forgeries, was substantiated by a British Parliamentary investigation looking into British intelligence prior to the start of the war. Ironically, the forged documents (discussed above) indicating an Iraqi-Niger yellowcake connection were a bit of a "red herring". The British Government report in fact, establishes an ongoing, three year relationship between principals of these two nations for purchase of uranium by Iraq from Niger. The

---

[185] Senate Intelligence Committee Report, 43.

report stated, regarding the accuracy of intelligence indicating a relationship between Niger and Iraq:

> In early 1999, Iraqi officials visited a number of African countries, including Niger. The visit was detected by intelligence and some details were subsequently confirmed by Iraq. The purpose of the visit was not immediately known. But uranium ore accounts for almost three-quarters of Niger's exports. Putting this together with past Iraqi purchase of uranium ore from Niger, the limitations faced by the Iraq regime on access to indigenous uranium ore and other evidences of Iraq seeking to restart its nuclear programme, the JIC judged that Iraqi purchase of uranium ore could have been the subject of discussions and noted in an assessment in December 2000 that . . . "unconfirmed intelligence indicates Iraqi interest in acquiring uranium (JIC, 1 December 2000).

> We conclude that, on the basis of the intelligence assessment at the time, covering both Niger and the Democratic Republic of Congo, the statements on Iraqi attempts to buy uranium from Africa in the Government's dossier, and by the Prime Minister in the House of Commons, were well-founded. By extension we conclude also that the statement in President Bush's State of the Union Address of 28 January 2003 that "The British Government has learned that Saddam Hussein recently sought significant quantities of uranium from Africa" was well founded.[186]

Regarding published allegations by former Ambassador Joseph Wilson and his conclusions that President Bush "lied" to the American people regarding the potential sale of yellowcake by Niger to Iraq, the Senate report concluded:

---

[186] Report of a Committee of Privy Counselors, *Review of Intelligence on Weapons of Mass Destruction*, House of Commons, July 14, 2004.

- That substantial intelligence existed indicating that Iraq was not only attempting to buy yellowcake from Niger, but also the Democratic Republic of the Congo and Somalia.[187] The Senate report also states, despite Mr. Wilson's statements to the contrary, "For most analysts, the information in (Mr. Wilson's) report lent more credibility to the original CIA reports on the uranium deal."

- Mr. Wilson misrepresented himself when he told *The Washington Post* he knew the Niger intelligence had been based on forged documents. The CIA did not obtain the document alleged to be a forgery until eight months after Mr. Wilson's return from Niger and allegations of the forgery surfaced a year after his return. "Committee staff asked how the former ambassador could have come to the conclusion that 'the dates were wrong and the names were wrong' when he had never seen the CIA reports and had no knowledge of what names and dates were in the reports."[188]

Both the British Parliament and US Senate reports underscore Mr. Wilson's inconsistencies on this issue and the fact that both the President and Vice-President were unaware of potential intelligence problems, even though the Vice-President had specifically questioned the accuracy of the CIA's conclusions on the subject.[189] Cogema[190], a French corporation, owned both of the yellowcake uranium producing mines involved in these investigations.

**Third Myth**. Vice President Dick Cheney misled the nation by stating that Iraq was involved in the 9-11 attack.

---

[187] Senate Intelligence Committee Report, 125.
[188] Ibid., 45 and 125.
[189] Jack Kelley, "Yellowcake Twists", *The Washington Times*, July 20, 2004.
[190] *BBC*, "Niger Upset by Uranium Slur, July 14, 2004, http://news.bbc.co.uk/2/hi/africa/3065165.stm. Accessed October 21, 2005.

**Truth**. On September 14, 2003, Tim Russert interviewed Cheney on *NBC's Meet the Press*. The exchange included the following:[191]

> Russert: The *Washington Post* asked the American people about Saddam Hussein, and this is what they said: 69 percent said he was involved in the 9-11 attack. Are you surprised by that?
>
> Cheney: No I think it's not surprising that people make that connection.
>
> Russert: But is there a connection?
>
> Cheney: We don't know. You and I talked about this two years ago. I can remember you asking me this question just a few days after the original attack. At the time I said no, we didn't have any evidence of that. Subsequent to that, we've learned a couple of things. We learned more and more that there was a relationship between Iraq and al Qaeda that stretched back through most of the decade of the '90s; that it involved training, for example, on BW (biological weapons) and CW (chemical weapons), that al Qaeda sent personnel to Baghdad to get trained on the systems that are involved, the Iraqis providing bomb-making expertise and advice to the al Qaeda organization . . . With respect to 9-11, of course, we've had the story that's been public out there. The Czechs alleged that Mohamed Atta, the lead attacker, met in Prague with a senior Iraqi intelligence official five months before the attack, but we've never been able to develop any more of that yet either in terms of confirming or discrediting it. We just don't know.

In his response, Cheney summarized the sketchy knowledge of Czech intelligence contention that Atta, the apparent 9-11 cell

---

[191] Stephen F. Hayes, *The Connection* (New York: Harper Collins, 2004), 16-17.

group leader, met with Iraqi intelligence in Prague. The Vice President framed this allegation objectively, but after his appearance on the show, in media outlets, "Cheney was accused of lying, inventing facts, disregarding intelligence, and reviving discredited conspiracy theories."[192]

At this writing, reports continue to surface that Cheney stated Iraq was involved in the 9-11 attacks. An objective reading of what he said to Russert clearly indicates otherwise.

No discussion of this issue would be complete without a brief review of the Czech connection that Cheney mentioned in his interview with Russert. According to Stephen Hayes, in his book, *The Connection*, background to the alleged meetings between Iraqi intelligence and Atta really began several years before, with the US decision to move Radio Free Europe to Prague in 1994. In 1998, at the height of a year long tussle with Saddam over weapons inspectors, culminating in a short bombing campaign in December, the US decided to begin radio broadcasts into Iraq from a separate facility in Prague. Saddam took exception to the presence of the new radio station, and, apparently initiated a plot to have a suicide bomber drive a truck bomb into the Radio Free Europe / Radio Liberty facilities in Prague. Iraq's intelligence chief in Prague, Jabir Salim, defected to England, alerting British foreign intelligence of the plot. Salim's replacement was a well known and seasoned intelligence operative, Ahmed Khalil Ibrahim Samir al Ani. Ani quickly became active casing the Radio Free Europe facility – to the extent that Czech intelligence and Radio Free Europe security were very concerned.

In May 2000, Atta attempted to get to Prague from Hamburg (where he was a student) for a meeting with an unknown individual. He waited too long to obtain a visa, so he could only get as far as the international lounge at the Prague airport on May 30, but he stayed there for almost six hours and met with

---

[192] Ibid., 18.

203

someone, away from the prying eyes of security monitors. Atta returned on a bus with his new visa three days later and spent about 24 hours in Prague. From there, he flew to Newark, New Jersey. In April 2001, Czech intelligence officials received a tip that Ani was about to meet with a "student from Hamburg". Two separate meetings between them may have occurred on April 9, the first reported by a single Arab source, and a second observed by Czech intelligence outside the Radio Free Europe facilities. Upon observing Ani with the student (later identified as Atta), Czech authorities decided it was time to send Ani home before he attempted to blow up the building.

In the aftermath of 9-11, meetings between Atta and an Iraqi intelligence official leaked out. Czech officials confirmed the meetings, but the FBI wasn't so sure, although they had a three day gap in Atta's paper trail (including April 9), they had cell phone records indicating that his cell phone was in use in the US during the gap. However, the 9-11 hijackers were known to have shared cell phones, so this evidence is not conclusive.

The *New York Times* and *Newsweek* began to publish stories discounting the connection, while Czech officials stood by their story. For example, the *New York Times* reported "that Czech president Vaclav Havel 'quietly told the White House he has concluded that there is no evidence to confirm earlier reports' of the meeting."[193] Havel and Czech officials denied that the phone call was made. Regardless, the "official" story that the meetings never occurred became received truth among the media and politicians.

The Vice President, in his discussion with Russert summarized by saying, "we don't know". In fact, we do not know.

**Fourth Myth**: No credible connection between al Qaeda and Iraq has ever been made.

---

[193] Ibid., 149.

**Truth:** In November 2003, author Stephen F. Hayes revealed the contents of a memorandum written by Under Secretary of Defense Douglas Feith to Senators Pat Roberts and Jay Rockefeller of the Senate Intelligence Committee regarding the issue of Iraqi-al Qaeda links. Quotes below are from contents of the memorandum.[194]

Mahmdouh Mahmud Salim (a.k.a. Abu Hajer al-Iraqi), now in a New York prison, was described in court proceedings related to the August 1998 bombings of US embassies in Kenya and Tanzania as bin Laden's "best friend". According to CIA reporting dating back to the Clinton administration, bin Laden trusted him to serve as liaison with Saddam's regime and tasked him with procurement of weapons of mass destruction for al Qaeda. FBI reports reveal that Abu Hajer "visited Iraq in early 1995" and "had a good relationship with Iraqi intelligence. Sometime before mid-1995 he went on an al Qaeda mission to discuss unspecified cooperation with the Iraqi government.

Reporting from a well placed source disclosed that bin Laden was receiving training on bomb making from IIS's (Iraqi Intelligence Service) principal technical expert on making sophisticated explosives, Brigadier Salim al_Ahmed. Brigadier Salim was observed at bin Laden's farm in Khartoum in Sept.-Oct. 1995 and again in July 1996, in the company of the Director of Iraqi Intelligence, Mani abd-al-Rashid al-Tikriti.

During a custodial interview, Ibn al-Shaykh al_Libi (a senior al Qaeda operative) said he was told by an al Qaeda associate that he was tasked to travel to Iraq (1998) to establish a relationship with Iraqi intelligence to obtain

---

[194] Quotes extracted from article by Stephen F. Hayes, "Case Closed", November 24, 2003, www.weeklystandard.com/Content/Public/ Articles/000/000/003/378fmxyz.asp. Accessed August 30, 2005.

poisons and gases training. After the *USS Cole* bombing in 2000, two al Qaeda operatives were sent to Iraq for CBW-related (chemical and biological weapons) training beginning in December 2000. Iraqi intelligence was "encouraged" after the embassy and *USS Cole* bombings to provide this training.

Sensitive reporting indicates senior terrorist planner and close al Qaeda associate al Zarqawi has had an operational alliance with Iraqi officials. As of Oct. 2002, al Zarqawi maintained contacts with the IIS to procure weapons and explosives, including surface-to-air missiles from an IIS officer in Baghdad. According to sensitive reporting, al Zarqawi was setting up sleeper cells in Baghdad to be activated in case of a U.S. occupation of the city, suggesting his operational cooperation with the Iraqis may have deepened in recent months. Such cooperation could include IIS provision of a secure operating bases (sic) and steady access to arms and explosives in preparation for a possible U.S. invasion. Al Zarqawi's procurements from the Iraqis also could support al Qaeda operations against the U.S. or its allies elsewhere.

Reference to procurement of false passports from Iraq and offers of safe haven previously have surfaced in CIA source reporting considered reliable. Intelligence reports to date have maintained A that Iraqi support for al Qaeda usually involved providing training, obtaining passports, and offers of refuge. This report adds to that list by including weapons and money. This assistance would make sense in the aftermath of 9-11.

According to a sensitive reporting (from) a "regular and reliable source," (Ayman al) Zawahiri, a senior al Qaeda operative, visited Baghdad and met with the Iraqi Vice President on 3 February 1998. The goal of the visit was to arrange for coordination between Iraq and bin Laden and establish camps in an-Nasiriyah and Iraqi Kurdistan under the leadership of Abdul Aziz.

Hayes also reported the following in his article,

> The day after (President Clinton's speech at the Pentagon on February 18, 1998), according to documents unearthed in April 2003 in the Iraqi Intelligence headquarters, by journalists Mitch Potter and Inigo Gilmore, Hussein's intelligence service wrote a memo detailing coming meetings with a bin Laden representative traveling to Baghdad. Each reference to bin Laden had been covered by liquid paper that, when revealed, exposed a plan to increase cooperation between Iraq and al Qaeda. According to that memo, the IIS agreed to pay for "all the travel and hotel costs inside Iraq to gain the knowledge of the message from bin Laden and to convey to his envoy an oral message from us to bin Laden."[195]

While the 9-11 Commission was conducting their inquiry and preparing their report, the Commission staff issued a series of "Staff Reports". Staff Report #15 includes the following statement.

> Bin Laden also explored possible cooperation with Iraq during his time in Sudan, despite his opposition to Hussein's secular regime. Bin Laden had in fact at one time sponsored anti-Saddam Islamists in Iraqi Kurdistan. The Sudanese, to protect their own ties with Iraq, reportedly persuaded bin Laden to cease this support and arranged for contacts between Iraq and al Qaeda. A senior Iraqi intelligence officer reportedly made three visits to Sudan, finally meeting bin Laden in 1994. Bin Laden is said to have requested space to establish training camps, as well as assistance in procuring weapons, but Iraq apparently never responded. There have been reports that contacts between Iraq and al

---

[195] Ibid.

Qaeda also occurred after bin Laden had returned to Afghanistan, but they do not appear to have resulted in a collaborative relationship. Two senior bin Laden associates have adamantly denied that any ties exited between al Qaeda and Iraq. We have no credible evidence that Iraq and al Qaeda cooperated on attacks against the United States.

The last statement above is usually seized upon and generalized by critics of the war in Iraq to mean no ties between al Qaeda and Iraq ever existed.

The Senate Intelligence Committee Report also addressed the issue of al Qaeda and Iraqi connections. It surveyed a number of individual reports and the degree of reliability assessed for each report among the intelligence community. The Report recorded a large number of reports and incidents including potential offers of safe haven from Iraq to al Qaeda, the use of training facilities, Hussein's knowledge of al Zarqawi's presence in Baghdad in 2002, Hussein's knowledge of al Qaeda presence in northeast Iraq, etc. The overwhelming weight of various reports supports a general conclusion that some level of cooperation existed between Iraq and al Qaeda during the 1990's and even after 9-11.

Media outlets ran stories about connections between al Qaeda and Iraq during the 1990's. For example, *Newsweek* magazine ran an article in its January 11, 1999 issue entitled "Saddam + Bin Laden?" It included:

Saddam Hussein, who has a long record of supporting terrorism, is trying to rebuild his intelligence network overseas – assets that would allow him to establish a terrorism network, US sources say he is reaching out to Islamic terrorists, including some who may be linked to Osama bin Laden, the wealthy Saudi exile accused of masterminding the bombing of two US embassies in Africa last summer.

Four days later on January 15, 1999, *ABC News* reported that three intelligence agencies believed that Saddam had offered asylum to bin Laden.

> Intelligence sources say bin Laden's long relationship with the Iraqis began as he helped Sudan's fundamentalist government in their efforts to acquire weapons of mass destruction . . . *ABC News* had learned that in December, an Iraqi intelligence chief named Faruq Hijazi, now Iraq's ambassador to Turkey, made a secret trip to Afghanistan to meet with bin Laden. Three intelligence agencies tell *ABC News* they cannot be certain what was discussed, but almost certainly, they say, bin Laden has been told he would be welcome in Baghdad.

However, after the invasion of Iraq, the media began contributing to the myth. The *New York Times* ran a story on June 9, 2003 entitled "Captives Deny Qaeda Worked with Baghdad". The story contended that captured high level al Qaeda operatives, including KSM and Abu Zubaydah stated in intelligence debriefings that they had no knowledge of a relationship between al Qaeda and Iraq. In the case of KSM (as pointed out in the Senate Intelligence Committee Report), he only went to work for al Qaeda later, and may not have had access to information about associations with Iraq. Abu Zubaydah reportedly said that bin Laden had misgivings about working with Saddam, which was likely, but would not necessarily hinder mutual support activities, as reports have alleged. What the *Times* did not report was that other senior al Qaeda officials, notably Ibn al Shaykh al Libi provided highly credible information that ties between al Qaeda and Iraq did exist, and actually accelerated after the al Qaeda bombings in Africa and attack on the *USS Cole*. The *Times'* story was picked by news outlets across the country and used as proof of Bush's duplicity in creating reasons for going to war in Iraq.

**Fifth Myth**: Iraq is not connected to any terrorists or terrorist activities.

**Truth**: This myth was repeated by Cindy Sheehan in a statement listed in Chapter Eight. In fact, Saddam and his regime can be easily linked to several terrorist organizations and/or activities.

Saddam paid families of Palestinian suicide bombers out of funds generated from his UN "Oil for Food" scam.

Saddam housed Abu Nidal until his death in Baghdad in 2002. Abu Nidal's terrorist organization conducted a wide range of activities in 20 countries claiming about 900 victims. He operated against the United States, Israel, Britain, France, the PLO (with whom he split in 1972), Austria, Turkey, Greece, and Jordan (among others). Iraqi secret police claimed that Nidal had died from taking his own life while being arrested for espionage on behalf of Kuwait.

Saddam maintained a warm relationship with the Palestinian Liberation Organization (despite Nidal's presence in Baghdad) over the years. The *Iraqi News Agency* reported in a story dated July 10, 1997 the contents of a note sent to Saddam from Yasir Arafat which included, "greetings of the Palestinian president to President Saddam Hussein and reiterated the Palestinian people's pride in their close relations with the Iraqi people and in the principled and firm Iraqi positions in the face of challenges and conspiracies implemented by the enemies of the Arab nation."

Abu Abbas, the Palestinian terrorist responsible for the 1985 hijacking of the liner *Achille Lauro* and the death of American tourist Leon Klinghoffer, also took up residence in Iraq in 1994 under Saddam's protection. Abbas was the Secretary General of the Palestinian Liberation Front. He was detained by US forces in Baghdad in April 2003, but died of a heart attack in Iraqi custody in March 2004.

In addition, the Iraqi government under Hussein was involved in terrorist activities, including the gassing of 5,000 of

210

their own citizens and the attempted assassination of former President George H. W. Bush in 1993. The planned method of attack was to blow up a Toyota Landcruiser packed with about 90 kilograms of explosives.

**Sixth Myth**: Minority US soldiers are being killed in Iraq at a disproportionately larger rate than white soldiers.

**Fact**: In January 2003, Representatives John Conyers and Charles Wrangle introduced legislation in Congress to reinstate the draft. One stated reason for the proposed legislation was that African American and Latino soldiers were dying at a higher rate than white soldiers in the "War on Terror". This allegation replays a widely held myth from Vietnam for a new generation of American youth and their uninformed elders. According to a story in the *Los Angeles Times* by Tony Perry on September 24, 2005, a Pentagon study revealed the following racial breakout of casualties from Iraq, based on a survey of killed and wounded as of May 28, 2005:

| Racial Makeup | % represented in Armed Forces in Iraq | % of the total killed |
|---|---|---|
| White | 67% | 71% |
| African-American | 17% | 9% |
| Hispanics | 9% | 10% |
| Asian / Pacific Islanders | 3% | 3% |
| American Indian / Alaskan | 1% | 1% |
| Multiple or Unknown | 3% | 6% |

This recent Defense Department study did not look at the economic background or rank structure in this study, only racial makeup.

211

# Illustrations

# Figure 2 - Operation Just Cause, Panama, 1989

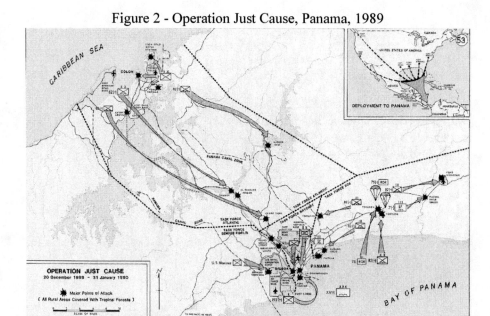

(*Westpoint Atlas*, United States Military Academy)

# Figure 3 - Operation Desert Storm, 1991

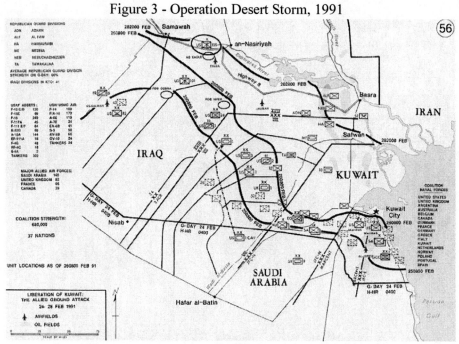

(*Westpoint Atlas*, United States Military Academy)

214

Figure 4 – Operation Iraqi Freedom, 2003

(Department of Defense Briefing Slide, Situation as of April 4, 2003)

# Index

Defense Intelligence Agency
(DIA), 107, 194, 195, 198
Duarte, President Jose Napoleon,
58, 59, 60
Dukakis, Governor Michael, 55
Dutch Battalion, 123, 124, 127
East Germany, 54-56, 60, 62, 71,
74, 79, 91, 92
Eden, Prime Minister Anthony,
33, 34
Egypt, 32-43, 47, 48, 89, 96, 99,
103, 104, 108, 186
Eisenhower, President Dwight D.,
3, 33, 34
El Salvador, 58, 59, 61, 67
Federal Bureau of Investigation
(FBI), 48, 137, 145, 147, 204,
205
*Fedayeen*, 164, 166-171, 177
Fonda, Jane, 19-22
France, 1, 18, 32, 34, 45, 69, 71,
97, 104, 130, 141, 159, 161-
163, 210
Franks, General Fred, 104, 107
Franks, General Tommy, 164-166,
169
Galloway, Joe, 9
Garrison, Major General William,
117, 118
Glaspie, Ambassador April, 98, 99
Gorbachev, President Mikhail, 56,
81-83, 85-87, 90-94, 185
Gorelick, Deputy Attorney
General Jamie, 146
Great Society, 8, 19, 26, 36
Greece, 71, 79, 141, 210
Grenada, 50, 55, 60, 61, 67, 85
*Gulf of Tonkin Resolution* (or
*Tonkin Gulf Resolution*), 5-7,
192
Hanson, Victor Davis, 11, 12, 150,
182
Harkin, Senator Tom, 56
*Hezbollah* 46, 58
Ho Chi Minh, 1, 2, 3, 5
Hussein, Saddam, 49, 96, 98-103,
105, 107, 108, 110-113, 128-
130, 132, 135, 150, 152, 158-
166, 170-174, 176, 179, 194-
198, 200, 202-205, 207-210

Iran, 40-44, 46, 47, 49, 57, 58, 72,
78, 88 89, 95, 96-98, 100, 110,
123, 134, 145, 148, 149, 158,
186, 195
Iraq, 30, 32, 34, 45, 58, 95-112,
116, 128-135, 138, 139, 145,
148, 158-166, 168-180, 183,
184, 186, 194-211
Israel, 30, 32-40, 45, 46, 47, 49,
58, 95, 96, 98, 100, 107, 159,
163, 186, 210
Italy, 31, 69, 71, 97, 122, 124,
141, 161, 162, 168
Izetbegovic, President Alijo, 123
Jennings, Peter, 56, 57, 176
Johnson, President Lyndon B., 4,
6-9, 15, 19, 25, 26, 35, 36, 186,
192
Jordan, Eason, 173, 174
Jordan, Kingdom of, (also, Trans-
Jordan) 30, 32, 35-39, 45, 96,
210
Keegan, John, 162, 167, 168, 171,
173
Kennan, George, 3, 69, 70, 152
Kennedy, President John, 3, 4, 5,
17, 28, 144, 148
Kenya, 137, 138, 205
Kerry, Senator John, 19, 20, 21,
26, 27, 56, 184, 196
KGB, 19, 20, 51, 53, 54, 61, 85
Khalid Sheikh Mohammed
(KSM), 149, 209
Khobar Towers, 134, 138, 139
Khomeini, Ayatollah Ruholla, 41,
42, 44, 75
King, Martin Luther. 19
Kissinger, Secretary of State
Henry, 38, 39, 71
Kosovo, 140-143
Kosovo Liberation Army (KLA),
140-142
Kurds, 95, 96, 98, 111, 162, 195
Kuwait, 96-100, 102-106, 108-
110, 129, 130, 135, 158, 163,
165, 210
Lawrence, Thomas Edward (T.
E.), 30, 95
Lebanon, 30, 32, 38, 45-47, 58,
134, 144, 180, 186
Liberation Theology, 51-53

217